FIRST IMPRESSIONS

FIRST
IMPRESSIONS

What You Don't Know About
How Others See You

ANN DEMARAIS, PH.D.,
AND VALERIE WHITE, PH.D.

BANTAM BOOKS
New York   Toronto   London   Sydney   Auckland

FIRST IMPRESSIONS
WHAT YOU DON'T KNOW ABOUT HOW OTHERS SEE YOU
A Bantam Book / March 2004

Published by
Bantam Dell
A Division of Random House, Inc.
New York, New York

Book design by Patrice Sheridan

Library of Congress Cataloging in Publication Data is on file with the publisher.

ISBN: 0-553-80320-4

Manufactured in the United States of America
Published simultaneously in Canada

10 9 8 7 6 5 4 3 2 1
BVG

IN MEMORY OF TIM O'BRIAN

Contents

Acknowledgments

First and foremost we want to thank Lesley Alderman for her ongoing conceptual insight and excellent editorial advice. She helped us translate psychological and business concepts into accessible ideas. We couldn't have written this without her. We'd also like to thank our agent, Jennifer Gates, for encouraging us to write this book and nurturing us through the process, and our editor, Danielle Perez, for her thoughtful advice.

Many friends and family members read numerous drafts; their comments were invaluable in the creation of the final book. In particular, we'd like to thank Heidi Peterson, David Halvorsen, Therese Reichert, Eileen Duffy, Thomas Morelli, Ira Noveck, Andrea Newman, Kristin White, Barry Cohen, Amy Sohnen, Michael Rohrer, Robert Demarais, and Terri Demarais. We also want to thank our business colleagues and the consultants of First Impressions, Inc., especially Eyal Pavell, John Motay, and Charles Hymes, for sharing their keen observations and insights. We are grateful to Marianne Gillow, who was particularly helpful in the development of First Impressions, Inc.

Colby Kant and Claudia Marks were fabulous research assistants. And Michael Sagristano provided a careful review of the psychological research. Thanks for your help. We also want to give many thanks to our clients for being so open to feedback and personal development.

FIRST IMPRESSIONS

Introduction

Imagine you are sitting at a bar with your best friend, who is about your age, similarly attractive, and intelligent. You both strike up a conversation with the bartender. You're all laughing and having a good time. But as the conversation goes on you realize the bartender is paying much more attention to your friend than to you. You feel hurt, and a little confused.

At your spouse's company party you meet many new people and are generally having a good time. On the way home, you have an uneasy feeling that you may have made a fool of yourself. You ask yourself whether you talked too much, told too many jokes, or were rude to the boss's wife. You question your husband closely, and he assures you that you were, in fact, charming and entertaining. But you still feel uncertain.

You're on an airplane flying from California to Chicago. The woman sitting next to you is interesting and engaging. You talk about the business trips you are returning from, your ex-spouses, and your favorite restaurants. You both admit you are single and hate the dating scene. At the baggage claim you exchange phone numbers. Yet when you call your traveling companion a few days later, she doesn't return the call.

Encounters like these occur all the time. We meet people whom we like, want to work or socialize with, but who don't seem to return our interest. We leave parties worrying about what people thought of us.

Though these meetings and the impressions we leave may seem fleeting, they can often have a far-reaching impact on our lives. An impression is important in the sense that there is a "retained remembrance," a lasting sense of someone or something. A first impression is our first and sometimes only opportunity to provide someone with a sense of who we are—a sense that will most likely be a lasting one. This is one of the reasons why first impressions are so crucial in terms of how others will view you and whether they will want to get to know you better.

First impressions is a topic of classic interest, and also particularly timely in today's world. For centuries people stayed in the communities in which they were born. They formed relationships, socialized, and conducted business with people they knew their whole lives. Now, however, we live in an age in which people move to new houses and cities, change jobs, make new friends, and form new relationships at a more rapid rate. First meetings happen so frequently, we hardly even register them. We might interact with someone new every day—another parent at our child's school, a new coworker or client, a store clerk, someone at the gym or in line at a coffee shop.

In these encounters, we may talk about the weather or what's going on in our lives and develop an initial understanding of others. Based on this very brief interaction, these strangers will form an opinion of us and probably will decide whether they like us or not. Whether we are perceived as sincere, interesting, or fun will determine whether others will be attracted to talk with us again, hire us, socialize with us, or date us.

Wouldn't you like to know what people are thinking about you?

This book will help you answer the questions "How do others see me?" "What do they see beyond my physical presence?" and "How can I make a better impression?" We provide the information you need to answer these questions by outlining the relationship between what you say and do and how others will likely perceive you. We've found that these relationships are extremely simple, but not always intuitive, even to the intelligent and well educated. While this knowledge is critical to success in life, it isn't taught in school, and rarely does anyone tell you this information honestly and objectively.

OUR EXPERIENCE

Our expertise in first impressions stems from our many years evaluating and coaching leaders and managers in Fortune 100 companies. We interact with professionals in role plays or "simulated" business situations, such as meeting a new client, and observe the way they present themselves and manage the conversation. We then provide feedback on the effectiveness of their communication, their sensitivity toward others, and the clarity of their ideas, among other things. Over the years we noticed that intelligent, competent executives were often unaware of the effect that they had on other people. Understanding the nuances of their communication style was invaluable to these business professionals in improving their effectiveness in the workplace and in their overall relationships with others.

After some experience with this work, it became clear to us that *everyone* could benefit from this kind of personal, objective feedback. However, it was available only to professionals in large corporations or to patients in psychiatric hospitals who needed to learn very basic social skills. There was no service available for average people to learn what type of first impression they made. So we decided to fill that gap and founded a unique business, First Impressions, Inc., in New York City.

At First Impressions, Inc., we use the same methodology, but focus on the social world. We go on a "simulated date" or social meeting with clients in a café, and, while interacting, observe their interpersonal styles and manner of self-presentation. Following the "date," clients join us in our office for a feedback session. We ask them what they intended to project about themselves and how they thought they came across to their date. We compare their beliefs to our perceptions, and provide them with specific supportive and constructive feedback.

This method is extremely effective in both the business and social worlds in helping people learn about themselves, and our clients love getting this kind of feedback. Most clients report that they learned things about themselves that no one had ever pointed out to them before. They also discovered that by changing what seemed *to them* to be a small or insignificant behavior, they received much more positive reactions from others.

In this book we show you what we show our clients. We deconstruct a first impression into its seven fundamentals—accessibility, showing interest, conversational topics, self-disclosure, dynamics, perspective, and sex appeal—and help you see how you come across in each element.

OUR CLIENTS

Our points are illustrated with client examples, drawing on the experiences we have had working with clients from all walks of life—old and young, male and female, outgoing and shy, straight and gay. We provide three kinds of examples:

1. *Business clients.* Some of these examples come from simulated meetings and feedback sessions. Others are from our direct experiences meeting clients for the first time and then speaking to them about their self-presentation. And several examples are taken from business situations that our clients have recounted to us.

2. *First Impressions, Inc., clients.* When on a simulated date with a client, a consultant goes by the name of "Susan" or "Nick." "Nick" and "Susan" are actually psychologists, but present

themselves as nonpsychologists, using past professions for their "aliases" when conversing with their dates. Throughout the book, when you see "Susan" and "Nick," it indicates a First Impressions, Inc., consultant on a simulated date.

3. *Everyday encounters.* These examples are taken from common social situations—at parties, airports, and the like—that clients, friends, and colleagues have shared with us or that we've personally experienced or observed.

Names and identifying information about people used in the examples have been changed.

We use business, dating, and social situations to illustrate the fundamentals of first impressions in a variety of contexts—and to highlight the fact that your style of presenting yourself transcends situations. The context matters, of course, and will determine the subject matter of what you discuss. For example, you probably talk about your personal interests in a social situation and address business issues with a new client. But in general, regardless of the situation, people form a first impression of you more by your style, such as how you show interest in them, navigate topics, and self-disclose, than by the content of your discussion.

OUR APPROACH

Our approach is different from other self-help books in that we make no prescriptions about how people "should" present themselves. There is no one "right" first impression or "right" way to communicate. *A good first impression is one that reflects the real you. If you are presenting the best of yourself, the self you want to share, then you are making the impression that is right for you.*

We aim to inform you, not to change who you are. You may learn that you come across in a way that isn't widely appealing but be okay with it. For example, you may find out that you come across as cynical or negative, but not want to change that because you like a cynical edge and like others who share that style. What we do is help you identify gaps between how you think you come across and how others actually perceive you, so you can make changes *if you want to* and *when you want to*. Of course, we respect that you may not want to impress everyone you cross paths with. But with a little knowledge, you can make positive impressions effortlessly and automatically.

We acknowledge that few people strive to please everyone—aside from politicians, that is. There are individual differences in what people like and seek out in others. But at the same time, there are "universals"—elements of interpersonal style that are more broadly appealing than others. For instance, most people like those who listen well and are entertaining and interesting. Focusing on these universals will help you understand what aspects of your style are broadly appealing and which of your behaviors are not universally appealing—so you can be aware of the messages you send and anticipate favorable or unfavorable reactions from others.

These universals are just that, behaviors that are appropriate and attractive for everyone, no matter their age, physical appearance, socioeconomic status, sexual orientation, or race. For that reason, in our examples we focus on what our clients say and do, not their demographic characteristics. Most of these universals transcend gender. For example, smiling, showing interest, and taking turns when speaking are attractive and common behaviors in both men and women. Where there are gender differences, we point them out. For instance, men have a greater tendency to present factual information in a first meeting—what we call "male-patterned lecturing."

Where first impression behaviors do vary, however, is among cultures. There are many cultural differences in what is considered normal and engaging in first meetings. What's appealing in Japan is much different from what's appealing in Brazil. While we acknowledge this, we are going to concentrate on the norms in American culture.

Our focus is on one-on-one, face-to-face interactions in social, business, and everyday situations, such as meeting new colleagues, first dates, and talking to strangers at a party. We address the first conversation you have with someone—not just the first few seconds of sight. We focus on your psychological first impression—that is, what kind of person you present yourself to be—rather than your physical first impression—what you convey with your physical appearance and style. Of course, appearance matters in how others perceive you, but how you react to others and present yourself matters even more, and will enhance or detract from your physical presentation.

THE BENEFITS TO YOU

You may be thinking, Okay, I could make some changes in the way I present myself to make a really great first impression, but why should I bother? Sure, I meet new people, but I am who I am. I don't want to change that. My friends and colleagues like me as I am.

The most important reason to understand the first impression you make is that it may not accurately reflect who you are—that is, how you really know yourself to be, or how your close friends see you. You may be misperceived in ways that you are not aware of. For example, if you are shy, you may come across as aloof; if you are very talkative, you may come across as self-absorbed. Meeting new people can cause even the most confident people some anxiety, stemming from uncertainty about being liked and accepted. New people haven't spent enough time with you to know and love you for all your positive qualities, and will therefore form an opinion based on limited information, such as your body language and style of conversing.

If you know you are making the impression you desire, you have the peace of mind that you have presented an accurate picture of yourself to others. If you are accepted or rejected, it will be because of your real qualities, not because you were misrepresenting who you are. You can gain control over whether and how relationships develop. If you tweak your style, people may respond to you more positively, and you may get more pleasure out of everyday encounters. You can become more confident in new situations. You may even be able to transform a neutral or negative interaction into a more mutually satisfying one and have more compassion and acceptance for people who may make common first impression miscommunications.

WHAT YOU MAY NOT KNOW

You don't always see yourself as others do. Some people see themselves as less interesting and appealing than others see them. However, many people put a favorable spin on their personalities and personal presentation. It's easy to overlook your own shortcomings. In our experience, most people send many appropriate and positive messages yet have a few "blind spots," areas where they send unintended messages that put others off.

Before you read further, take the following short self-evaluation. Read through this list of behaviors and reflect on whether each is something you do usually, sometimes, or rarely. Check the box that fits your self-impression.

Do you think about the messages that these behaviors convey to others? Typically, the first four send positive messages, and the latter four can send negative ones. In Part II, The Seven Fundamentals of a First Impression, we'll explain these behaviors, and how they make others feel, in more depth.

Tables like this are included at the end of each of the chapters in Part II. They provide a great opportunity for you to assess your own behavior. The more you use these tables, making checks and notes, the more you will be able to understand the patterns of your unique first impression style.

FIRST IMPRESSION BEHAVIORS

When I meet someone new, do I:	Usually	Sometimes	Rarely
Smile and lean toward others when they are speaking?			
Talk at the same speed as my conversational partner?			
Show comfort with my body?			
Share a sensitive area or vulnerability?			
Volunteer impressive information about myself that I would like others to know?			
Start a conversation with what is currently on my mind?			
Focus on presenting my unique features?			
Try to communicate my social or financial success?			

HOW THIS BOOK IS STRUCTURED

Part I is about the psychology of first impressions—how they are formed, what people look for, and why they are so important. Part II outlines the seven first impression fundamentals. And Part III shows you how to synthesize what you've learned and actually make changes to your first impression style.

WAYS TO READ THIS BOOK

There are two ways to read this book. They're both good. If you're like us, and think psychology is fascinating, you'll want to read the book in the order presented, by starting with the Psychology section, then moving on to the specifics in the Fundamentals section. If you are more into the practical or are especially eager to learn about yourself, you can skip the Psychology section and move right to the core of the book—Part II: The Seven Fundamentals of a First Impression. You can go back to the Psychology section later.

TIPS ON HOW TO GET THE MOST FROM THIS BOOK

1. *Open your mind to seeing yourself in an objective, nonjudgmental way.* Focus on yourself, not on evaluating or changing others. It's always much easier to see "first impression faults" in others than to see them in yourself. We all know "somebody else" who talks too much or goes into way too much detail. As you are reading through the examples, you'll probably quickly connect a flaw with someone you know. But, as others are reading this book, an example may remind them of something about you, something you may continue to overlook if you don't reflect and consider yourself. If you get used to the idea that you, like everyone, can at times be an "annoying somebody else," you'll learn much more.

2. *Self-assess as you go.* We present a lot of information, so it's helpful to think about each section and self-assess before moving on to the next chapter. Use the tables provided to check whether you do each behavior usually, sometimes, or rarely. Some people don't like writing in books. If you're one of them, you can print the tables from our web site: www.FirstImpressionsConsulting .com. It's important to note the things you do well, and be confident in those strengths, as well as behaviors that may send the wrong messages. Then we'll review your self-assessments in Part III: Tweaking Your First Impression Style, and refer back to those tables to pull out the one or two things overall that you would like to improve.

3. *Apply what you learn right away!* Try out what you learn the

next time you are in a new situation. You may find that even fine tunings will result in very different reactions. Our hope is that by the time you have finished this book, you will already be noticing changes in the way others react to you in day-to-day situations. We also hope that you will feel more confident and comfortable in your ability to make the impression you want, from innocuous encounters to an all-important meeting. In the process, you will become a better and more sensitive judge of others.

4. *Read this book with a friend.* You can read one chapter, and pass it to your book buddy. Then for each chapter, ask your friend to point out a few things you do really well and one thing you could do better. Of course, you want to be sensitive when you share your impressions—see more tips in Chapter 11. Sharing this experience with a friend as you read the book will help you see the gaps between your self-perception and how others see you.

The Psychology of First Impressions

What's really going on in people's minds when they meet someone new? What do they notice? What are they thinking about? If you knew that, you would have a much better idea of the impression you make.

While we can't make you a mind reader, we can illuminate some very common ways people process information about others, so that you can have more insight into how people form an impression of you as a person.

The psychology of first impressions is simple, but not always obvious. In this section we outline these simple psychological processes. Chapter 1 describes how people form impressions—that is, how people take a small sample of you and use that to filter all future information about you. Chapter 2 shows you the emotional underpinnings of first impressions, and specifically how focusing on what others are feeling about themselves is the secret to making a positive first impression. And Chapter 3 presents the key benefits that people seek out in social interactions—feeling appreciated, connected, elevated, and enlightened—and how providing them makes you more appealing to others.

This section is for the psychologically interested. If you'd like to skip the theory, you can jump to Part II, where we show you the specific and practical aspects of first impressions.

How First Impressions Are Formed

You're in the waiting room at your dentist's office. A woman walks in and takes a seat next to you. She smiles and strikes up a conversation. She talks about the *People* magazine cover story, and comments on how quiet the waiting room tends to be—considering what's going on inside. She asks you about yourself and tells you a story about something that happened to her earlier in the day. You realize that you really enjoy this woman's company; she's fun and easy to talk to. You can imagine being friends with her. Ten minutes later you are called into the office, and you say good-bye.

Have you ever had a similar encounter? One where you met someone very briefly and were left with the feeling that you had a sense of that person? Just by the way she spoke and how she responded to you, you got a feeling about who she is. Maybe you imagined you knew her lifestyle or values, could predict what she is like in other situations, and had a good idea of whether you'd enjoy her company in the future.

From a brief interaction you created a rich understanding of someone you just met.

How did this happen? How did you take a small amount of information and create a much larger picture? Knowing the psychology of first impressions—how it works and how you can use it—can give you a guide to deciding how you want to present yourself.

In a first impression, others see only a little sample of you, a tiny percentage of your life. But to them, that sample represents 100 percent of what they know of you. While you've had a lifetime of experiences with yourself—you know the full range of your emotions, behaviors, passions, and fears—strangers don't know anything about you at all. That tiny sample of you is all they have to work with, yet they will unconsciously assume that the sample is an accurate representation of all of you.

Think about the woman from the dentist's office that we just introduced. She was chatty, lively, and observant. At that moment. But because that's the only experience you have with her, you will assume that is how she'd be all the time. Why would you think any differently?

Psychological research has shown that people weigh initial information much more heavily than later information when they evaluate people. It's a simple fact: The first information people get about anything—a person, a place, an idea—influences the way they process later information. In other words, people are more likely to believe that the first things they learn are the truth.

For example, if you show a warm interest in people on a first meeting, as the woman in the waiting room did, they may form an impression of you as an engaging and connecting person, and not notice or not care later if you are distracted or self-absorbed. Negative initial information is weighted even more heavily. If you initially appear distracted and self-absorbed, others may ignore your later warmth and interest for a very long time. It can take many positive behaviors to overcome the impact of *one* initial negative behavior.

THE FILTER

A first impression is like a filter. Here's how others form an image of you:

1. People take in initial information—they notice your body language, what you say, and how you respond.
2. Based on this initial information, they form an impression and make decisions about what you are like and how they expect you to behave in the future.
3. They then see you through this filter. Everyone likes to think they are a good judge of character, and think "I knew from the first moment I met him that he was..." They seek information that is consistent with their first impression and will not look for, or even will ignore, behavior that doesn't fit their impression of you.

FILTERING ERRORS

Personality or Situation?

While the filter allows people to make sense of information quickly, there are some common errors in the process. For example, people tend to see a new person's behavior as indicative of that person's character or personality in all situations, when it may not be. If you meet someone who seems angry, you may think he is an angry person in general. You may not stop to consider whether something has just happened to make him act that way. Maybe someone just cut him off on the road or he just got some bad news. This is a fundamental error that we all make; we tend to see others' behavior as indicative of their personalities, or characters, in all situations, rather than the result of a temporary external situation. However, that's not how we tend to see our *own* behavior. When we are angry, we probably attribute it to the situation, not to our personality trait.

Halo and Horns

Another error people make is assuming that a person with one positive trait also has a cluster of other positive traits that he or she may
not have. For example, you may assume that someone who appears
upbeat is also smart, likable, and successful, even though you've never
seen evidence of those qualities in her. This is called the "halo effect."
People also tend to see negative traits in the same manner—the
"horns effect." For example, we may assume that someone who complains a lot is also boring, unsociable, and weak.

If you understand these common errors of perception, you can better
understand how others form an impression of you on a first meeting.
And you can be in a better position to present an accurate image of
yourself. If you know that others will assume that the tiny percentage
of you that they first observe reflects 100 percent of your personality,
then you can be careful about what information you present. Realizing
that order matters, you may want to show your best qualities *before*
your less charming ones. Knowing that people tend to assume you
have a cluster of traits based on a single behavior, you may want to
choose the cluster of traits you'll be placed in. In other words, if you
know how you will be perceived and categorized, you can better control the impression you make and ensure that it represents your real
self.

TWO

How You Make Others Feel

Perhaps you can remember an interaction with someone who made you feel really good about yourself, when you felt respected, valued, and understood. Now try to remember a time when someone's words or actions made you feel bad about yourself—insulted, unappealing, or alienated.

Do you think about how others feel about themselves after they speak with you? You should. Because what you say and do impacts the way people feel about themselves. How people feel after interacting with you on a first encounter is especially important, because it will impact how they feel about you, at that moment and perhaps permanently. It's straightforward: If you make people feel understood and happy, they may project that good feeling onto you and feel positively about you. However, if you inadvertently insult them or make them feel ill at ease, they may project inaccurate negative traits onto you. At the very least, they will associate their good or bad feelings with you.

This chapter shows you how these emotions come to play in even very short interactions and explains the different ways you may focus your emotions. Chapter 3 describes more specifically what it means to make others feel good in a first meeting—that is, satisfying the core things people seek out from social interactions: appreciation, connection, mood elevation, and enlightenment. Part II elaborates how specific behaviors communicate these feelings and satisfy core desires in others.

FOUR WAYS TO FOCUS

David, a First Impressions client, is a Wall Street analyst. He was chatting with "Susan" at a café. In the course of their conversation, David told Susan about his interest in the history of New York City and a class he was taking on the subject. He told her about a paper he was writing on the political history of the city. Susan complimented him on his initiative and insights. She said she would be interested in reading his paper. He expounded on some of the key points in his essay. David liked Susan; Susan made him feel good about himself, respected for his ideas, and understood.

Because of her expressed interest and respect for him, David naturally assumed that Susan liked him. But what David didn't think about was how Susan was feeling or how she was feeling about herself. When the consultant asked him about this in the feedback session, David admitted he didn't really think about that directly during the simulated date. But, since he felt good, he assumed that she did too. The consultant pointed out that she, as "Susan," felt informed by David's ideas, but she also felt that David didn't care about her very much because he never showed any interest in her, never asked her about herself or her opinions, and made no effort to connect with her.

David's misunderstanding is a common one. We often assume that if we are having a good time that the person with us must be enjoying herself too. That's because, when you meet someone for the first time, you often focus on what you say and what you talk about. But how you come across to others is less about what you say or how you feel and more about how you make people feel about themselves in your presence. Every first interaction, even a casual conversation with a stranger on the street or at a party, can have an emotional impact on both individuals.

There is a simple way to look at the different emotions involved. An interaction can affect:

1. How you feel about yourself
2. How you feel about the other person
3. How the other person feels about you
4. How the other person feels about himself or herself

FOCUS 1: HOW YOU FEEL
ABOUT YOURSELF

This is a common focus in new situations. You talk to someone at a party or a meeting, and you notice how you feel—whether you are comfortable, energized, bored, nervous, intimidated, and so on. It's normal, unavoidable, and, of course, interesting and important to us all. It guides how you interact with people, what situations you seek out, and whom you choose to associate with. In this example, David felt confident, understood, and informative, and wanted to continue talking to Susan.

FOCUS 2: HOW YOU FEEL
ABOUT THE OTHER PERSON

Once you feel comfortable enough with a new situation and a new person, you commonly relax your self-focus and turn your emotional attention to how you feel about others. You evaluate others based on how they respond to you and what they say and do. You make quick decisions about their personality, how much you like them, and so on. As discussed in Chapter 1, this is a natural, and often unconscious, phenomenon. David quickly noticed that he liked Susan; he felt that she shared his ideas and attitudes.

FOCUS 3: HOW THE OTHER PERSON FEELS ABOUT YOU

Making a good impression means making someone feel positively about you—so how the other person feels about you should be an important focus. And it usually is when you are in situations in which you consciously want to impress someone or know you are being evaluated—such as in a first contact with a client or a first date. During the interaction, you may notice whether the other person smiles and pays attention to you, laughs at your jokes, and seems engaged. Or you may reflect later and try to evaluate the kind of impression you made. David didn't think about how Susan felt about him. He was caught up in thinking about how he felt.

FOCUS 4: HOW THE OTHER PERSON FEELS ABOUT HIM- OR HERSELF

You may not realize how powerfully you can affect how others feel and, especially, how they feel about themselves. Sure, you know that you can entertain or bore someone, but do you think about how you can make that person feel proud or insightful? It's important, because how people feel about themselves after interacting with you will impact how they feel about you. Focus 4 is the most neglected of the four emotional focuses. Do you typically think about your emotional impact on others? Do others leave the conversation feeling really good about themselves?

When you are with people you know well, you may readily perceive how they are feeling—and strive to make them feel good. For example, you may compliment a friend on his fine cooking because you know it's important to him and you want him to feel proud. However, in a first conversation, you may not think about how others feel about themselves. That may be because you don't know them and can't tap in to their emotional needs easily. And, in the discomfort of a first meeting, you may be distracted by your own feelings and needs.

We've noticed that our clients are much more oriented to Focus 1, 2, and 3 than to Focus 4.

An orientation toward Focus 4—how others feel about themselves— is the secret to making a positive first impression. But it's not obvious because it's not an automatic emotional orientation. It doesn't just pop into your awareness the way feelings about yourself do. It re- quires conscious thought and shifting of attention. But if you *can* shift your focus from your own feelings to making others feel good, you'll be more likely to make a better first impression. For example, David ne- glected to think about how Susan was feeling and how she was feeling about herself. As a result, he didn't make the impression he thought he was making or get the reaction he expected. We've seen that a lot of misunderstandings stem from a neglect of Focus 4.

Self-Check:

Where is my emotional focus when I meet someone for the first time? Do I think about how I feel? Or do I think about how others are feeling about themselves?

After You: Social Generosity

Focus 4 is a form of social generosity. It's what is commonly meant by being "nice." It's putting others' needs and feelings before your own. While relationships are about mutual need fulfillment, *first impres- sions are about meeting others' needs.* When you meet someone for the first time, it's a short but special moment. When you put your own needs aside for that moment and shift your focus to the other, you demonstrate that you can be generous and selfless. If you don't, it may suggest that you can't and that you may be an emotional burden, someone who is draining to be around. It's like telling strangers that you are interested only in yourself or that you have some unsatisfied needs that you're hoping they can fulfill.

THE BALANCE SHEET

Being socially generous has advantages in the world. People unconsciously evaluate you by the social benefits you provide and balance them against any social "costs" you incur. According to the theory of social exchange, people seek out others who provide them with the feelings and benefits they desire and people who provide them with the most benefits are the most desired. So, if you make others feel special and put them in a good mood, you will be more socially desirable than others who don't provide them with such positive feelings. You make yourself less desirable if you incur social "costs"—that is, if you deny others the benefits they seek by failing to show your appreciation, putting them in a negative mood, or boring them.

An important feature of social exchange is that it *is* an exchange. We evaluate, and are evaluated by, the benefits we provide to others. It may sound cold, but it explains a lot of human behavior. And to ignore this fact is to miss out on an important part of normal and healthy human dynamics.

As when looking for a friend, a spouse, or an employer, you like to feel that you're getting the most you can. Everyone likes being with someone they enjoy, who is good to them, respects them, and has a minimum of burdensome qualities. Think of someone you especially like to be around. What social benefits does that person provide? How does he or she make you feel? Think of someone who is socially difficult. What costs does he or she incur?

GETTING WHAT *YOU* WANT

If you spend all your energy making the other person feel good, what about you? How can you be sure you get what you want? Although you may not have thought about it clearly (until now), you probably have a feeling of what you would like to get out of interactions with others. You may like to be around people who make you laugh. You may like to share a lot about yourself because it makes you feel understood, or you may enjoy talking about your work because it allows you to feel talented. How do you balance getting what you want while focusing your energy on others?

Paradoxically, the shortest route to getting what you want is to give to others first. It's true. The more you listen and connect, the more likely it is that others will return the attention. A first interaction may be an opportunity for two people to experience a pleasant moment, or it may be the start of a friendship, social connection, business relationship, or romance. If you begin from a position of generosity, and meet others' needs, you lay the groundwork for getting reciprocal fulfillment. Your act of social generosity will endear you to others and open the door to acceptance. It gives you more power to pursue the relationships you want—and you can decide later whether you are getting back what you want or need.

THREE

The Four Universal Social Gifts

Now you know the value of focusing on how others feel. But you may not know specifically *how* to be socially generous. What do people want exactly?

While people vary in what they desire and need from others, there are some important social gifts that are universal. They are: appreciation, connection, elevation, and enlightenment. If you know which you are giving or not giving, you'll have a good idea of the impression you make.

APPRECIATION

Everyone likes to feel appreciated and affirmed. You show appreciation when you let someone know that you understand and respect her for her positive qualities. For example, if you tell someone directly or indirectly that she is talented, funny, smart, or attractive, she will feel proud about that quality in herself and good about herself in general.

Our client, Nancy, a 30-something paralegal, told us about a pleasant encounter she had with Dean, a 30ish architect, whom she had met at the party of a mutual friend. In the course of conversation, Nancy was lucky to receive most of the four social gifts.

Here's how Dean showed his appreciation for Nancy:

NANCY: I used to not exercise at all, but I started taking karate classes last year, just for the activity. Now I love it, and I just became a green belt.

DEAN: That's quite an accomplishment! I know a lot of people who put off starting something they want to try, and now you look like you're in great shape, *and* have a green belt—a force to be reckoned with!

CONNECTION

Connection is about finding where you intersect with someone. It can be a mutual friend, common interests, or similar experiences. It can be as simple as pointing out where you have the same attitude or feeling about something, as in "I feel the same way," or "I loved that movie too." In essence it's saying "I'm like you." People like it because it makes them feel understood and provides them with a sense of belonging.

Here's how Dean showed a connection to Nancy:

NANCY: I really like detective stories and books about true crime, thrillers, and the like.

DEAN: Me too! I love John Grisham, James Patterson, and Sue Grafton. Have you read them? A few friends and I pass these books on to each other. I'll send some your way if you like.

ELEVATION

People naturally like to be in good spirits, to laugh, and feel uplifted—and are drawn to those who make them feel that way. You don't have to be a comedian. You can elevate others' moods in many ways, such as by smiling, being in the moment, acting playful or entertaining, and directing your attention to the positive and humorous elements in the situation.

Here's how Dean was able to improve Nancy's mood:

NANCY: Man, it's freezing outside. I just hate this weather, I feel like I can never get warm.

DEAN: I know what you mean. It's like the North Pole! But you just gotta love the snow, it's so clean and refreshing. It's so quiet in the city when it snows. Wasn't it pretty last night when it was falling?

ENLIGHTENMENT

We're all curious. We like to learn something new—interesting facts, ideas and perspectives, current events, even trivia. Bearing the gift of enlightenment makes you stimulating and appealing to be around. It doesn't have to be about some heady book you read or international politics—it can be about the curious thing you noticed on the way to work, the movie you just saw, or an article you read in a magazine.

Here's how Dean enlightened Nancy:

NANCY: What did you do today?

DEAN: Nothing special, puttered around the house. But get this, I watched this TV program about World War II. Did you know that during the war, the Japanese sent a whole flotilla of hot air balloons across the Pacific to bomb America? Most landed in the mountains. . . .

NANCY: Hot air balloons, wow, no, I didn't know that.

Here Dean was able to extract an interesting fact from his day and enlighten Nancy at the same time.

That's all there is to it. You can make others feel good after interacting with you if you appreciate them for who they are, connect to them, elevate their mood, and stimulate them with new ideas and perspectives. And these social gifts transcend situations. It's true that specific situations have different expected benefits. What is appropriate on a first date may be different from what is appropriate in a business meeting. But it's a matter of proportion. In a romantic one-on-one interaction, you may desire, and wish to fulfill, feelings of appreciation and connection. You may also like to have fun and be informed about the other's ideas. In a business interaction, on the other hand, information plays a bigger role, but the other benefits are still important. A customer who appreciates you and makes you laugh is certainly appealing.

THE IMPORTANCE OF BALANCE

A healthy balance of the four social gifts is charismatic. On the other hand, an imbalance can be off-putting. For example, David, the Wall Street analyst described in the previous chapter, was quite enlightening. During his first date he informed Susan of what he learned in a course he was taking on New York City history. He shared his insights and ideas. Yet he didn't show any appreciation for Susan and didn't find a way to connect with her or amuse her. While David focused on the one gift of enlightenment, Susan focused on all the things she felt deprived of. The imbalance was very glaring to Susan and made David much less appealing than he would have been if he gave a balance of social gifts.

People have personal preferences, of course, for what they seek out from others. For example, some may really like to be entertained and seek out those that make them laugh, and not care that much about feeling connected to people. Others may especially enjoy feeling understood and love talking with people who make them feel that way, and not care much about being enlightened. However, you usually don't know this about people you meet for the first time. So balance is good strategy.

WHAT DO YOU GIVE?

So what social gifts do you give? This is, in effect, the fundamental question of this book. Maybe you never thought of yourself as giving or denying something in a first impression. But you do. Do you satisfy others' desires for the things that they, like you, desire in a social interaction? Do you deny others the opportunity to satisfy some desires? Do you offer a balance of the four social gifts?

We recognize that most of us have a "strong suit." Maybe you have a quick wit and are highly entertaining. Or perhaps you are well informed and like to tell others about current events and your opinions. But maybe you have some weak suits as well. You may not be aware of the feelings and social gifts that you fail to give to others or of any emotional costs you may incur. Would you like to give not only your strengths, but also the other desirable social benefits? Knowing what you want to give can help you understand if there are any gaps between what you would like to project and how others actually see you. Of course, you may elect not to offer all these gifts; it may not be your style. But it's helpful to be aware of what you do and don't give to others. If you know how others feel when they interact with you, you'll have a better sense of how they perceive you.

Self-Check:

What benefits do I provide to others? Do I have a strong suit? Of all the social benefits—appreciation, connection, elevation, and enlightenment—which am I strongest in? How would others describe how they feel after a conversation with me? Are there any gifts that I tend not to give to others?

SUMMARY

People form impressions of you quickly and unconsciously. They make assumptions about you based on the initial things you say and do, and then see you through the filter of these initial assumptions. They assume that your first behaviors represent how you act most of the time, even if it is not true. Based on the first things you do, they may attribute other positive or negative traits to you, even those they haven't actually observed.

Making a positive first impression is straightforward. The secret is focusing on how others are feeling and especially how they are feeling about *themselves*. If you can shift your focus to the other person, you can better satisfy their needs. Keep in mind that, while relationships are about mutual need fulfillment, *first impressions are about meeting others' needs*. You satisfy their needs when you show appreciation for their positive qualities, make them feel connected, put them in an elevated mood, and enlighten them with information and ideas. Remember, when you are socially generous, others are more likely to return the attention and satisfy your social desires.

In Part II we show how these psychological principles play out in the real world and outline the seven fundamentals of first impressions and the specific behaviors that communicate them.

PART TWO

The Seven Fundamentals of a First Impression

We take in and integrate information about people in a fast and usually unconscious manner. But what specifically are people looking for and reacting to when they meet someone for the first time? What provides the positive and negative feelings that so strongly affect their judgments?

A first impression is a small and intricate puzzle. But if you take it apart, you can see each piece clearly and how it fits into the whole. Then you can put the pieces back together again with a better understanding of how the impression was created.

In this section we take a first impression apart into its seven basic pieces. These fundamentals are: accessibility, showing interest, the subject matter of first conversations, self-disclosure, conversational dynamics, perspective, and sex appeal. If you take your own first impression puzzle apart, you can see how you come across in each of the seven fundamentals. Piece by piece, you can gain a nuanced understanding of the way you are perceived by others.

To help you understand these first impression fundamentals, we provide examples of what our clients do and then challenge you to ask yourself "Do I do that?" We share research findings that show how specific behaviors influence impressions. At the end of each fundamentals chapter, we summarize the behaviors in a table where you can ask yourself whether a behavior is something you do usually, sometimes, or rarely.

In Part III, "Tweaking Your First Impression Style," the pieces are put back together again, so you can create a comprehensive picture of the way others see you. We'll show you how to synthesize the information and identify behaviors that you'd like to change to make an impression that better reflects the way you see yourself, the real and best you.

FOUR

Opening the Door: Accessibility

Have you ever been alone at a party scanning the room for someone who seemed open to talking with you? Or have you ever been in a strange city looking around the street for someone of whom you can ask directions? You probably don't pick someone randomly. You evaluate people by how open they seem to contact. You pick up on subtle cues they are sending out.

You also send these cues, ones that say "stay away" or "I'm safe and approachable." Whether you know it or not, you have a style that tells others how open you are to them. You show it by the way you hold your body, how you hold their gaze, and how you respond and engage with them. Are you aware of how open you make yourself to contact? In general, do people seem comfortable striking up a conversation with you at parties? Do map-carrying out-of-towners seem to pick *you* to ask where they can find the closest subway? Do people banter with you in elevators?

Naturally, you might not want to be approached by strangers most of the time—especially if you live in a crowded city. But sometimes you may want to appear inviting. Perhaps you'd enjoy a casual conversation with someone in a waiting room, an airplane seatmate, or an intriguing guest at a party. So it's helpful to know how to make yourself more accessible so you can draw others to you, when you want to.

Your "accessibility style" is important because it literally determines whether an interaction takes place at all. It also affects the *quality* of the interaction if it does occur. Even before you speak with someone, your own comfort level affects how the other person feels in your presence. You can make him feel relaxed or anxious, confident or insecure. You may not realize your "power from a distance." But you have it, and if you understand it, you can harness it. You can use that power to make others feel comfortable around you, which will likely bring out their own best qualities and a better interaction with you.

The first fundamental of a first impression, then, is how you make yourself open to others. There are two key components of your accessibility. The first is your style of making contact: whether you take the initiative to introduce yourself, what mood you project, and how actively you set a comfortable tone. The second component is content—what you actually say when you begin an interaction.

Some of the behaviors addressed here will be discussed in more detail in later chapters, so you will encounter them again as we move deeper into decoding the first impression puzzle. Here the focus is on just the very first stage of a first impression.

YOUR ACCESSIBILITY STYLE

How do you invite contact? Think about a time when you wanted to speak with someone and wanted him or her to come to you or respond to you. Perhaps it was at a party or a conference. What did you do, how did you appear?

The Art of Being Approachable

Strangers may take in a lot of information—how you move, how you talk, how you engage with others—before they ever actually meet or speak with you. Your apparent openness filters the way others see you. It's the prequel to a first impression.

Consider one of our business clients, Theo. He arrived at a cocktail party at one of our training sessions with some of his colleagues. Theo chatted with his colleagues who were laughing and telling stories about some past escapades. But Theo had heard most of these stories before and felt bored. He noticed that the other guests at the event looked interesting, and he wanted to talk to some of them. He sipped his Heineken, hoping that someone would approach him. But he slowly noticed that people were gravitating more toward his colleagues than to him. He felt excluded, and slightly bewildered.

Theo was unknowingly sending out messages that he wasn't a comfortable person to approach. Specifically, we observed that his body language was not engaging—he had a rigid posture, made little eye contact with others, and wasn't responding to people. Others sensed this and chose to approach "easier" targets—his cohorts who seemed fun and open. Theo was interested in contact and thought he appeared open. When he tried to jump into the conversation, others seemed not to respond to him. He had no idea that his body language was keeping others away and filtering the way others saw him even before he spoke.

Self-Check:

Do I appear open and interested, or closed and withdrawn? What do I do to send out these messages? What do strangers infer about me based on my body language?

Body Talk

Let's look at the details. What are the important elements of body language that draw or put off people? Theo, for example, was not smiling, had a stiff posture, and wasn't looking at people. He didn't seem "present" and open. Instead he seemed distant and self-contained. All of these behaviors were deterrents to people approaching him.

What could Theo have done differently? For starters, he could have smiled. We are certainly not the first to point out this important element, but we can reinforce what you already know: A smile tells the world that, at that moment, you are happy or pleased. When you smile at people, they consciously or unconsciously feel that you find them appealing. It's an invitation to contact. This is one area in which we actually recommend that our clients force something. If they smile and show pleasure in inviting or greeting someone, they make the other person feel better about him- or herself and facilitate a better interaction. While the lack of a smile may feel neutral, and even more natural, to you, it actually sends an unintended negative message that you are not attracted to or interested in the other or that you have an unpleasant disposition. Theo wasn't smiling because he was bored. But others didn't know that.

Self-Check:

Do I make an effort to smile when I meet new people or am in a new situation, even if I am uncomfortable?

What else could Theo have done? He could have relaxed his body. Holding your body in a relaxed posture generally makes others feel comfortable and invited. He could also have made eye contact with others. By making eye contact and nodding toward someone, you send positive feelings and make yourself more approachable.

Theo wasn't aware of what his body was doing. It's hard to know, and we certainly can't see ourselves the way others can. One good way to learn about this is to ask a trusted friend to tell you what messages they see in your body language.

MOST LIKE IT HOT

People who come across as warm are typically viewed as less threatening than their aloof or cold counterparts. But what does it mean to be "warm"?

To understand the elements of body language that send these "temperature" messages, researchers videotaped participants as they engaged in a five-minute conversation with someone. They asked each participant to rate how warm or cold they thought they came across. Then they showed a silent videotape of the interaction to others, "the observers," and asked them to rate the conversationalists in the same way.

For observers, the body language that indicated warmth was showing physical attention, smiling, and nodding. The body language that indicated coldness was not attending to others, not smiling, and extending their leg (while seated).

Interestingly, the people being rated didn't see these behaviors as indicating coldness in themselves. They had no idea that they were seen that way.

So, you may want to pay attention to your temperature signals. Others may judge you as cold, even though you don't feel that way, or intend to send that message. And then people may respond to you negatively, while you remain what the researchers call "unpleasantly mystified" by these reactions.*

*Various research studies are referred to throughout the book. More information about these studies can be found in the reference section on page 223.

Risk Management

Everyone fears rejection. It's part of the human condition. When you appear "safe" to others, you minimize this fear and make yourself seem welcoming. For example, you are usually less risky to approach at a party when you are standing alone than when engaged in an intimate conversation with someone—because there are fewer obstacles to engaging you. You appear less risky, even if you are chatting with someone, if you have an open posture and create space for someone else to join.

You are also less risky when you appear to be similar to others—not superior or very different. When you seem similar, others feel more certain of what to expect from you and more certain that you will understand each other and connect. However, being "safe" is not about conforming and giving up your sense of self. Instead it's about *adapting* to others and the situation. If you adapt to the immediate social environment—whether it's a hoedown or a black-tie benefit—you will make yourself more approachable. You convey your similarity in the way you dress and groom, of course, but also by the way you speak and respond to others. That may simply mean showing interest in the topics of the other guests, expressing appreciation for the music or food, and showing what you have in common with others—rather than focusing on your unique qualities or by presenting yourself as different.

Fitting In

Consider our business client Lauren, a sophisticated businesswoman from Los Angeles with a fashionable wardrobe and stylish tastes. Lauren relocated to a small city in the Southwest because she wanted to have a slower pace of life and more of a sense of community. While she loved her new city and the people there, she didn't feel welcome. Finally a colleague pointed out that her style of dressing and conversing made the local people feel that Lauren was putting on airs and that she felt herself to be superior to them. Lauren then tried making herself more approachable by dressing more casually, talking about local events, and taking more social initiative. Though it was uncomfortable for her at first—she wasn't used to wearing khakis and talking about ranching—she found it much easier to connect with her new neighbors and coworkers.

When you adapt to a local situation, it's affirming—it makes others feel comfortable with themselves and thus more comfortable around you. And it sends the message that you are like them and safe.

Looking Good

Appearances matter in first impressions. Your looks may be the first information a stranger has about you—and so they play a bigger role in a first meeting than they do in later meetings. Most of us are aware of this and make an extra effort to look good for an important first business meeting, party, or date. It's expected, and it can make a first meeting go smoothly. When you look good and appear comfortable with yourself, your appearance can then recede from attention, and others can focus on your personality and what you talk about.

Part of looking good is looking appropriate and fitting in, as we described with Lauren in the last example. Looking good also means taking care of yourself, showing style, and projecting confidence in your appearance.

When you show that you take care of yourself, it sends the message that you are healthy, respect yourself, and make an effort to be pleasing to others. Taking care includes being clean and neat, getting good dental care, and even trimming your nose hairs! When you neglect your appearance, it may suggest that you are socially unaware or careless.

Style matters too. Style includes dressing and grooming in a way that reflects your individuality and current trends. Having style sends the message that you are confident in yourself and tuned in to the world around you. Of course, some people are better than others at cultivating a personal style. If you are uncomfortable in this area, you could get some insight by paying attention to how people you admire present themselves, by asking a trusted friend for feedback, or even seeking the help of a style consultant.

Style is about projecting an accurate sense of yourself. Your style can tell an "instant story" about you—whether you are serious or fun, traditional or progressive. So you might want to be sure that you are telling the right story about yourself. If you sport the cotton-shirt-and-sneakers look, you may think you come across hip and casual, but others may think you're a nerd. If you wear tight-fitting clothes, you may think you look sexy, but actually come across as seeking attention. You may not be hitting the mark you're trying for. If you're just a little unsure, it can't hurt to ask a trusted friend for feedback.

And you don't have to be good-looking to look good. Beauty is nice, but confidence trumps. Even if you aren't blessed with movie-star good looks, if you show comfort with your body and appearance, others will too. If you are poised, no matter your bone structure, height, or weight, you will come across more positively than if you try to mask or compensate for a perceived flaw. You make yourself

---

THE SPOTLIGHT ILLUSION

When among strangers, we may at times overestimate the impact of the details of our appearance. Because we know ourselves so well, we might feel self-conscious about slight differences in how we look. We might feel unattractive be-cause our hair is a bit flat or we are wearing the wrong shoes, and think others are focused on these "flaws" too. But are we correct in our estimates of how others view us? The answer is: probably not.

Researchers have looked at whether people accurately assess the extent to which others take note of details of their appearance. In one study, participants were asked to wear T-shirts with images that they felt proud of or embarrassed by (such as a picture of Barry Manilow), and then walk into a roomful of strangers. They were then asked to estimate the percentage of people who would remember the image on their T-shirt after they left the room. The results showed that the participants consistently overestimated the number of people who recalled their T-shirt image.

In other words, people assume that the details of their ap-pearance are more memorable and remarkable to others than they actually are. The researchers concluded, "People tend to believe that the social spotlight shines more brightly on them than it really does."

more attractive when you show comfort in your own skin, and show pride rather than shame. Body comfort is addressed in more detail in Chapter 10.

Finally, think big picture. If you fit in, take care of yourself, and project style and confidence, you'll look good. Don't sweat the details; strangers probably won't notice your earrings or the color of your tie.

The First Opportunity

Aside from making yourself approachable with your body language and appearance, you also have a simple and straightforward opportunity in first encounters: to take an active or passive approach. It comes down to: Are you the introduced or the introducer?

Waiting for an Introduction: The Passive Approach

One of our clients, Jill, told us about an awkward experience she had had at a party hosted by a colleague. The only person Jill knew at the party was the hostess, who was busily greeting her many guests. Jill glanced around the room hoping to see a familiar face in the crowd. Seeing no one, she made her way to the buffet. Two women next to her in line were chatting with each other. As Jill filled her plate with food, she turned to the man standing next to her. The man nodded at her and then, reaching for a plate, turned away, leaving Jill feeling awkward and conspicuous. "Is there something wrong with me?" she wondered. "Am I dull or unattractive?" Jill then took her plate of food and found a spot where she could eat alone. She felt uncomfortable and began to think about how long she could tolerate the party.

You've probably been in a situation where, like Jill, you knew no one and didn't have an easy entrée to a conversation. You may have felt self-conscious, which may have made you less comfortable approaching someone. Like Jill, you may have misinterpreted others' casual behavior as a rejection, and let it ruin your mood.

Making the Introduction: The Active Approach

Let's imagine that Jill had handled her party situation a little differently.

Jill took her plate of food and looked around for a place to sit down. Seeing a few people on the other side of the room around a coffee table, she walked over, introduced herself, and sat down. She explained her connection to the hostess and asked them about themselves. Within a few minutes Jill was engrossed in a conversation; it turned out they all knew some people in common from Jill's previous employer. When a woman strolled by looking for a place to eat, Jill invited her to join them and introduced herself and her new acquaintances.

In this hypothetical scenario, Jill took an active approach and introduced herself. She took a risk. But she quickly found common ground with others and became less self-conscious. She sent the message of confidence and comfort, and drew people to her. Most people prefer those who show social initiative. It makes them feel comfortable and connected. And, importantly, it takes the burden off of them to make contact.

Of course, an active style does not guarantee that others will always include you in a conversation or group. Sometimes people are engaged in private conversations or not open to a new conversation. Nonetheless, in general, taking an active approach will make others more comfortable with you and likely lead to more and better interactions than a passive approach.

Self-Check:

Am I more comfortable as the introducer or the introduced? Can I take an active role in a new situation and introduce myself to strangers?

Creating the Tone

In addition to introducing yourself, you also have the power to create the tone of a first interaction. You can do that with the mood you project, as well as by how actively or passively you engage others.

What's Your Mood Quotient (MQ)?

Moods are infectious. Surely you've noticed the mood of strangers and how it can make you feel. You can interact with a waitress with a lighthearted style and leave the restaurant with a smile on your face. Or you can be upset by an angry post office clerk and go on to feel bitter all day, spilling your bitterness into your conversation with co-workers, putting them in a worse mood, and so on.

Whether you are aware of it or not, your mood changes people—how they feel about themselves, how they feel about you, and the way they respond to you. In every interaction, you transfer some of your mood to the people you talk to. And most people have a preference for what mood they like to receive from others: They are drawn to those who display a positive mood. That's because it makes them feel elevated (remember, one of the universal social gifts discussed earlier), and it lessens the feeling of threat or rejection.

The Elements of Your Mood Quotient Your mood is conveyed by your body and your words. At any given time, you have an MQ that is the combination of these factors:

- Physical energy
- Facial expression
- Emotional tone of speech
- Vocabulary—whether you use weak or powerful words
- Orientation of focus: positive or negative

THE WARP SPEED OF
EMOTIONAL EXPRESSION

Research has shown that people form certain impressions of others within a few seconds. In that time frame, people pick up on and respond to expressions of emotion, such as anger or pleasantness, that are conveyed to them through body movement, facial expressions, and eye contact.

And negative emotions travel faster than positive ones. Instinctively people have the fastest reactions to those who could be considered a threat, such as those who have angry expressions. This information is processed at a primitive neurological level, in a way that allows people to detect and react to danger. After they've scanned for danger, people's attention is drawn to those who appear safe and pleasant.

These primitive processes still play out in our civilized culture. While seeing a stranger scowl may not send you running for your life, you still have a fast and negative reaction to it. That's why it's good to be aware of what emotion you present in the very first seconds of meeting someone. While the grimace on your face may just be due to the traffic jam you just endured, strangers may notice it immediately, and register it as threatening and unwelcoming.

Miranda, one of our clients, is a 45-year-old account executive. She looked up slowly as her consultant approached her at the coffee buffet and said hello. She had a stern expression on her face and started the conversation by shaking her head and talking about how bland the coffee was, then went on to gripe about her company and her routine job responsibilities.

Later the consultant asked Miranda how she was feeling. Miranda responded that she felt fine, just a little tired, why did she ask? The consultant explained that she personally felt uncomfortable because

Miranda seemed to be in a bad mood. Miranda was surprised; she thought she was being straightforward. She didn't know that her "straightforward" style actually came across as a negative mood. Miranda was low on all of the components of the MQ: her energy level, lack of a smile, emotional tone, her weak adjectives (e.g., "bland" and "routine"), and her focus.

Miranda's consultant helped her see some consequences of conveying a low MQ. The first is the contagious effect: Her mood makes others feel more negative just by being in her presence. Second, some people may personalize the feeling—that is, feel that *they somehow elicited this negative vibe* in Miranda because she doesn't like them. Or third, people may feel that Miranda is always in a low mood and may reject her because they assume she will not be a pleasant person to be around in general.

What about you? Do you think about the fact that you have an MQ that you bring to every interaction? Of course your moods change depending on the situation, the time of day, and all sorts of other factors. But relative to others, you may generally be a very up or very down person. You can think of your MQ as being a number from 1 to 10, where 1 is a gust of arctic wind and 10 is a summer breeze.

When you meet someone for the first time, you may want to notice what mood you are projecting. Then see if you can stretch it up just one notch. For example, if you feel like you are coming across as a 4, see if you can try for a 5. It can be hard to change your mood on demand. But you can make small changes to the way you project it. You can try changing just one of the components.

Like smiling, mood is one of the few areas where we actually recommend our clients fake it—just a tad. It's a gift of social generosity, with a payback. When you are animated, you elevate others' moods. You make yourself more appealing to them and make yourself happier in the process.

How to Up Your Mood It could be as simple as smiling a fraction of an inch more or showing more energy. If you find it hard to be physically perky, you can try to compensate with language. Your use of descriptors can matter. Using superlatives, such as "incredible," "wonderful," or "beautiful" or even hyperbole, such as "I'd be happy if I stayed here for the rest of my life…" communicates a much more positive mood than descriptors such as "all right" or "nice." And be aware of the emotional tone in your speech. People are extremely sensitive to your emotional tone and will assume that it reflects your "true" feelings. If you say you are happy to see someone with a flat tone of voice, he will most likely conclude that you are not really all *that* happy to see him.

THE CHICKEN OR THE EGG?

As we all know, when you feel good, you smile. But did you know that if you smile, you feel good?

Psychologists call this "facial feedback." When you put your mouth into a smile position, you actually feel happier. Changes in facial expression can alter the temperature of the blood flowing to the brain and change the way you feel. Just curling up your lips can do it. In one study researchers had participants put a pen between their lips (which is like a frown) or between their teeth (like a smile) and then rate cartoons for funniness. Try it and see how it feels. Participants found the comics funnier when they were simulating a smile than when they were simulating a frown.

Self-Check:

Do I make an effort to present a slightly more positive mood? What is the easiest thing for me to change about my MQ: smiling more, using more positive language, or changing my emotional tone?

You May Already Do This—Some of the Time We've noticed that some people know how to project a positive mood yet don't make the effort—or recognize its importance—in all situations.

Take our First Impressions client Leonard, a successful real estate broker in his early 50s; he met his consultant in a downtown café for a late-afternoon coffee. Leonard arrived ten minutes late and was still visibly flustered when he got to the table. He explained that he had just had brunch uptown with some friends, but couldn't leave on time because the incompetent waiter wouldn't bring the check, and then on top of it, it was hard to find a cab, and someone cut them off at the light. After he vented these frustrations, he relaxed and jumped into a conversation with "Susan."

In the feedback session, his consultant brought up Leonard's negative opening. Leonard explained that he had these feelings and needed to talk about them; it was important to him. His consultant pointed out that *he* may have felt better afterward, but it didn't improve *her* mood, and it didn't make for a great first impression. Because she knew Leonard was a businessman, the consultant asked him if he would vent his frustrations when meeting a new client. He said absolutely not. He greets each with a smile and puts aside his personal issues. The consultant helped Leonard realize that he has the skill to put his own needs aside and can do so when he desires. In fact, he may be very good at it, and could apply that same professional skill in social first meetings. By treating social acquaintances with the same courtesy he treats his business clients, he would start with the same foundation of social generosity and warmth, and more likely bring out a better mood from his companion.

The Wait-and-See Approach

There are two parts to setting a tone. One is in the mood you project. The second is in how actively you engage your conversational partner. There are different ways to do that. We've noticed that some people prefer a passive approach. They don't create a tone, they let others do it for them. Then they decide how they feel, and if and how they want to engage.

While in general being reactive to others is a good thing, the wait-and-see approach can send an unintended negative message of disinterest or rejection.

Jerry, one of our First Impressions clients, met his consultant "Susan" for a simulated date one warm spring evening. Jerry is in his late 20s and works at a small architectural firm. When he arrived at the café, he took a seat across from Susan and said hello. Susan opened up the conversation by asking him about himself and what he did that day, one of the first warm days of the season. Jerry responded with a short answer. Susan felt the need to carry the conversation, so she told him about an interesting experience she had earlier in the day. Jerry listened attentively. Susan asked him another question, and getting little back, went on to talk about the movie she saw the previous night. Much later in the date, Jerry perked up and jumped into the conversation more actively. He told Susan about some interesting projects he was doing at work and about his family. But by this point Susan was frustrated with Jerry and had lost her enthusiasm for the connection.

Back at the office, the consultant asked Jerry about his reserved style. Jerry explained that when he meets new people, he hangs back and observes them to see how they address and respond to him. Then he decides how he feels about them and how comfortable he is around them. His consultant explained that while observing others is a good way to find an opening for connection, his *very* laid-back style sent the unintended message that he was uninterested in Susan, bored, or socially uncomfortable. While he is gathering information to decide whether he likes someone, he is simultaneously creating an environment that is not likely to bring out the best in others. *Not setting a positive tone is, in essence, setting a negative tone.* Jerry's lack of participation makes others sense that he doesn't like them, which makes them *less likely to like him.*

Jerry could have set a more positive tone simply by acting as if he expected to like Susan. He could have engaged her more readily by jumping into the conversation, responding to her questions, and showing energy with his body language—by smiling and leaning toward her. And he could have shown more interest in her and striven to find a comfortable dynamic. (These behaviors will be covered in more depth in Chapter 5 and Chapter 8.)

Self-Check:

Do I actively jump into interactions and create a welcoming tone, or do I sometimes hold back and wait for the others to make *me* comfortable before I warm up?

CONTENT: WHAT DO YOU SAY AFTER YOU SAY HELLO?

Now that we've covered your *style* of making yourself accessible—making yourself approachable to others, taking the step of introducing yourself, and setting the tone—we'll address what you actually say or talk about when you make your first contact with someone.

Striking Up a Conversation: The Moment Method

One of our clients, Jamal, a serious man in his early 40s, told us about an experience he had when he was invited to a birthday party for a colleague at a local restaurant. He was early for the dinner and decided to wait at the bar. He was standing close to a couple of people and had an easy opportunity to strike up a conversation, but felt at a loss about what to talk about. So he scanned the bar, looked at the paintings, looked at the other people, and listened to the music—and then had some fodder for a casual conversation. He turned to the woman beside him and introduced himself. Jamal explained that he was early to meet some friends and was just listening to the music. He said he thought it was a singer he used to like, whose name escaped him. His new acquaintance didn't know the singer either, but they talked about music and their favorite jazz singers for a few minutes, and then Jamal asked her some more about herself. They jumped into a lively conversation, one that was initiated by a simple remark about the music.

The most comfortable and expected subject matter of a first meeting is the immediate situation—the place and the people. If you can think of nothing to say, comment on something you see or hear. You can talk about the room, the weather, or the situation, with a smile and easy manner. When you are "in the moment," it is easy for others to respond to you because it connects to what they are simultaneously experiencing. It sends the message that you are socially aware, safe, and connecting. After this icebreaker, you can turn your focus to your conversational partner and what you have in common.

Self-Check:

Am I in the moment when I meet someone new? Can I find ways to open up conversations by connecting to the time and place, before jumping into a more personal or abstract discussion?

Note on Opening Lines

Since every environment is different, there is no specific opening line that is always appropriate. Being in the moment and being creative in what you talk about communicates that you are safe and fun. On the other hand, using prerehearsed opening lines can send the opposite message—that you are not safe or that you have an agenda.

Many books on mingling and "picking up girls" provide suggested opening lines, such as: "Can a beautiful girl like you use some pleasant company?" These opening lines, however, generally come across as "closing lines." Few people expect or desire seductive wit in a first encounter, and using such lines can send the message that you are shallow—or aggressive.

Opening a Prearranged Meeting

In a business situation, you don't have to find a way to strike up a conversation; you are meeting for a purpose. Nonetheless, you have a choice in how you open the conversation. And how positive you are the very first time you speak is important. If you start with a downer, you may have a very hard time pulling yourself back up in someone else's eyes. If you start with a positive comment, or at least a neutral one, you have a much better platform to work from.

Take the example of a business client of ours, Richard, a financial adviser who flew in from Phoenix for a meeting in New York. He walked confidently into the conference room and greeted his consultant with "Oh my God, this city is such a mess, every time I come here I can't believe it. The street was so packed someone even bumped into me." The consultant, a local, was a little taken aback, but politely acknowledged his perspective. Later Richard talked about how much he enjoyed his current work project. He went on to tell her about his great colleagues and how much fun he had with them. He also talked about how he was looking forward to meeting up with an old friend later in the evening.

Richard's consultant had a hard time warming up to him after he opened the conversation on such a negative note, even though he later talked warmly about people and situations in his life. When she brought this up with him, Richard explained that his opinions about the city were on the top of his mind when he met her and seemed like benign small talk to him. However, they weren't really benign—his negative comment biased the way she perceived him. Had Richard opened the conversation with a pleasant greeting—like "Wow, such energy in this city. It's amazing"—and then *later* mentioned his sidewalk experience, he would have made a much better impression.

The primacy effect is a basic of first impressions. The first information you see or learn about someone is weighted more heavily than what you learn later. You may know this basic principle but, like Richard, occasionally forget to check an impulse to share some negative thoughts when you meet someone for the first time. It's not that you shouldn't be honest; it's just that your travel difficulties, poor health, and pressing schedule are generally better saved for the second or third topic you bring up, rather than your opening line.

Self-Check:

Do I consider how opening topics might affect the impression I make? Do I suppress negative top-of-mind topics and open with a positive comment when I meet someone for the first time?

SUMMARY

Your openness to others is the *first* of a first impression. It can determine whether an interaction takes place at all and the quality of the interaction with someone, if and when it happens. When you appear engaged, welcoming, and safe, you invite contact and put others at ease.

Even though you can read others' subtle cues to accessibility, you might not know what cues you send. You may not be aware of how accessible you appear to others, or what it is that draws or deters them. It's hard to see yourself the way others see you, and any first impression jitters or insecurities may further distort your self-perception. But the signs of accessibility are relatively simple. You show your openness to contact with your body language—by smiling, making eye contact, and orienting yourself toward others. You make others more comfortable if you show your commonalities to them. If you are active and introduce yourself and set a positive tone for the interaction, you will likely foster a better interaction. Finally, you open up contact most easily by being in the moment and spontaneous.

How accessible do you appear to others? Do you know how to draw others to you when you want to? Do you make others feel safe

HANDSHAKE MESSAGES

A handshake is a common ritual in the introduction of two unacquainted people. Etiquette experts note that firmness, dryness, and temperature play an important role in impression formation.

Handshaking has also captured the attention of social psychologists, who have experimentally tested how the quality of a handshake impacts initial impressions. Their findings indicate that a firm handshake, characterized by strength, vigor, duration, eye contact, and completeness of grip, does have a positive impact on a person's first impression.

The researchers also looked at gender differences. They found that women with the firmest handshakes were seen as more confident and assertive, and made a more favorable impression on others, than women with a more "feminine" handshake. And surprisingly, women with firm handshakes were judged more positively than men with comparably firm handshakes.

Given this data, women might be wise to put their firmest handshake forward when meeting someone for the first time.

and comfortable around you? Take a moment to think about each of the behaviors in the following tables. Then make a check to indicate whether you do the behavior usually, sometimes, or rarely. It's really helpful to self-assess in this manner before moving on to the next chapter. In the conclusion, we'll show you how to synthesize self-assessments from the whole book into one or two behaviors you may want to work on.

POSITIVE ACCESSIBILITY BEHAVIORS*

If You Do This:	*You May Seem:*	*Do I Do This?*		
		Usually	Sometimes	Rarely
Smile when I meet someone	Inviting, affirming, likable, pleasant			
Adapt to the social situation and appear similar to others	Safe, comfortable, accepting, nonjudgmental			
Are well groomed, stylish, and comfortable with your appearance	Healthy, confident			
Introduce yourself and others	Engaged, socially skilled, comfortable			
Actively invite people to join you	Safe, welcoming, likable			
Create a positive mood and draw out others	Affirming, entertaining, comfortable to be around			
Open a conversation by being in the moment—talking about immediate situation	Safe, socially aware, easy to engage			

*All tables in this book can also be found on our web site: www.FirstImpressions Consulting.com.

COMMON MISCOMMUNICATIONS

If You Do This:	You May Think You Seem:	But You May Seem:	Do I Do This?		
			Usually	Sometimes	Rarely
Fail to smile	Neutral, thoughtful, cool	Uninterested or unattracted to the other, cold			
Focus on your individuality rather than your commonality with others	Interesting, eccentric	Inaccessible, self-involved, socially awkward			
Show little attention to your grooming and style	Natural, not concerned with superficialities	Socially unaware, careless			
Wait for an introduction	Neutral, unobtrusive	Distant, uncomfortable, uninviting, passive			
Observe and judge before interacting actively	Careful, thoughtful	Uninterested, difficult to connect with, aloof			
Use prepared opening lines	Charming, open, witty	Shallow, aggressive, calculating			
Open with a casual negative opinion	Straightforward	Unlikable, unpleasant			

FIVE

Enough about Me: Showing Interest

Making yourself open to others is the first fundamental of first impressions. It's critical to having an interaction. Once you've crossed that line and started a conversation, you're ready for the second fundamental: showing interest in others.

There are few hard and fast rules for making a positive first impression, but here's one: *You will come across more positively if you show genuine interest in people you meet for the first time.* While this may sound obvious, many of our clients, in the rush and pressure of a first meeting, lose track of this fundamental. But it's essential. People are highly attuned to others' interest in them. They feel it when it's there, and they feel it even more when it's missing.

Demonstrating interest in others says a few things about *you* as well. It says that you are open to connection and that you are not self-absorbed. It also says that you are secure in yourself and open-minded enough to seek to understand what lies beneath someone's surface appearance.

Think about it. Some of the best meetings you've had may have been ones in which you felt a connection to someone almost immediately, you felt comfortable and understood, and the conversation flowed easily. At the end of the meeting, you may have already been looking forward to seeing the person again. If you have had that kind of experience, then chances are you were with someone who was genuinely interested in you and who knew how to express that interest. Even if that person never said much about himself, the fact that he was so intrigued by you made you interested in him.

On the other hand, some of the worst interactions may have been with someone who never showed a modicum of interest in you, never asked you a question, or kept turning the conversation back to himself. You may have left such a conversation feeling exasperated and hoping not to see that person again.

When someone shows genuine interest in you, you feel appreciated and understood—a core social benefit that you seek out, and unconsciously react to, in interactions with people. You too have the power to shine this light on others. In fact, showing genuine interest is the easiest and most powerful way to make a good first impression. Just by being interested, you appear interesting.

In this chapter we outline the process and style of showing interest. The *process* is the way you direct your physical attention, ask questions, listen, and respond. Your *style* is how aggressively or passively you display your interest.

THE PROCESS: HOW YOU SHOW INTEREST

You show interest in others physically, by how you orient toward and look at them, and verbally, by how you address them, ask questions, listen, and respond. It sounds basic, but there are many nuances in the process. While you may be unaware of your subtle behaviors, others pick up on your messages very readily.

The Power of Physical Focus

A business client of ours, Eileen, is a successful manager in a large technology company. We observed her in a meeting where she was interacting with two of her new subordinates, John and Laurie. Eileen opened up the meeting with an overview of a new project and then invited input. Both John and Laurie eagerly shared ideas. However, in the course of the meeting, Eileen began orienting more toward Laurie. When Laurie presented her ideas, Eileen nodded, smiled, and leaned toward her. When John spoke, Eileen kept a neutral posture. Eventually John stopped contributing.

When Eileen's consultant pointed out this favoritism in the feedback session, Eileen was surprised. She noticed that John had "shut down," but had no idea that her body language had precipitated it. She felt that she was inviting input in a balanced way. Her consultant pointed out that while she was asking for ideas from both subordinates, her body language was very biased. The way she was physically focused on Laurie sent strong affirming messages to her yet simultaneously sent rejecting messages to John.

Our bodies reveal our interest. Often, like Eileen, we are more aware of what we say to others than how we physically communicate with them. As we mentioned in the previous chapter, the way we orient toward others when they are speaking, the way we move our heads, and the way we smile or fail to smile show others our degree of interest in them and what they have to say.

Self-Check:

Do I notice what my body conveys when I meet new people? Do I lean toward them, nod, smile? Do I consider how someone might feel if I don't attend to him to the same extent that I am attending to others?

Look at Me

Paul, one of our business clients, met his consultant at the office cafeteria for coffee. He quickly struck up a lively conversation with her.

He talked about his work and his career goals. He was interesting and positive. However, throughout the meeting, Paul kept looking away from his consultant. He would look just past her or around the room, as if he were distracted. Susan began to feel that Paul was bored or more interested in who was walking into the cafeteria than in her. She had a hard time connecting to him.

Later the consultant asked Paul if he had been distracted during the meeting. He said he felt fully engaged in the conversation and didn't mean to give that impression. When she explained that he made very weak eye contact, Paul said that he was totally unaware of it. He had no idea that he was sending the message of lack of interest.

It's basic. Eye contact is a clear indication of interest, especially in American culture. We normally look others in the eye most of the time we are talking to them. The rest of the time we may be looking at their mouths, other parts of their faces, or briefly away. Most people are aware of these norms and conform to them, sending messages that they are interested, honest, and comfortable to be around. If you make less eye contact than others, like Paul, you may unknowingly send messages of lack of interest or attraction, or social discomfort.

We've noticed that there is a small but significant percentage of people who make less eye contact than normal—but have no idea because they don't look at others long enough to know that they are deficient! We have worked with skilled businesspeople and socially adept First Impressions, Inc., clients who never knew they made poor eye contact.

If you know the norms and your own eye-contact pattern, you are in a position to control the messages you want to send. If you want to withdraw from someone, you can look at her less and make short gazes. And if you want to show interest or attraction, you can look at her more and hold your gaze longer, even *just a fraction of a second longer* than normal. Most people are very aware of being looked at and will feel this small difference—getting the message that you like them or find them appealing. Of course, staring, or 100 percent eye contact, especially from a man, can make people feel uncomfortable or threatened.

SHIFTY EYES

As we have noted, eye contact communicates your interest in others. But how much eye contact is expected and desired by others? What are the consequences of deviating from the norm?

Researchers investigated these questions and examined how much eye contact is typical in a face-to-face interaction. It turns out that most people make eye contact 45 to 60 percent of the time. They also studied what happens when people go above or below the norm. They asked participants to conduct a brief job interview with interviewees (really confederates) who were instructed to make high contact (90 percent of the time), normal contact (45 to 60 percent of the time), or low eye contact (10 percent of the time) with the interviewers.

The results indicated that those people who made low eye contact came across negatively in a number of ways. They were perceived as more superficial, less socially attractive, and less credible than people who made average or high eye contact. Interestingly, making a high level of eye contact didn't lead to more favorable impressions than making a normal amount.

Apart from what percentage of time you make eye contact, how long you hold a gaze has an impact on others. In another study, researchers found that people are more positively perceived if they make longer, less frequent gazes. When people made short, frequent gazes—the infamous "shifty eyes"— they were liked less.

From a first impression standpoint, you'll appear more socially attractive and likable if you make at least normal amounts of eye contact and hold your gaze.

Self-Check:

Do I make less eye contact than average? (Since this is hard to know about yourself, you may want to ask a close friend or family member for feedback.) Am I usually the first person to break eye contact? Try looking at people a little longer than you usually do, and see if they look away first.

The Ways You Voice Your Interest

In addition to your physical focus, you show your interest verbally, in the way you address people and ask, or fail to ask, others about themselves.

What's in a Name?
Ever notice that you can hear someone mention your name from across the room, even when you are in the midst of a conversation? Psychologists call this "the cocktail party effect." We can block out extraneous auditory information and focus on one conversation at a time. But some words—such as our own name—have the power to break through our perceptual filters. So even in the din of a cocktail party, if you hear your name, you perk up your ears.

Because your name is special to you, it gets through your perceptual filters more easily than other words and grabs your attention. In conversation, when someone uses your name, you have an unconscious, positive reaction to it. So likewise, if in a first meeting you use others' names, they may have an unconscious positive reaction and thus a positive reaction to you. It communicates that you paid enough attention to care, register, and remember it. How many times have you been introduced to someone at a party and forgotten her name the next second? It happens when you don't concentrate long enough to register it. If you remember a person's name, and use it once or twice on a first meeting, it generally makes a good impression. It may even be worth the effort to ask someone to repeat it or spell it.

However, there are a few caveats. Using people's names repeatedly can sound "salesy" and forced, especially in a one-on-one conversation where it's obvious whom you are addressing. And commenting about someone's name, especially if it's unusual, may be unappealing, even when you are genuinely curious and feel your comment is good spirited. Asking, "Jikuma? That's different. What kind of name is that?" can interrupt the conversational flow and force Jikuma to explain his ethnicity, something he may or may not care to talk about as a very first topic.

The Art of Asking Questions
Remember David, the client we described earlier? He is a Wall Street analyst who told his date "Susan" about his work and a class he was taking, and the topic of the paper he wrote. He was informative and stimulating. Yet in the course of the hour, David didn't ask Susan a single question about herself, her ideas, or her opinions.

This was what we call an imbalanced exchange of social gifts. In this case, Susan made David feel fulfilled by demonstrating that she appreciated and understood him. Susan, however, did not derive the same benefits from David and thus had a less positive experience. Although it sounds simple, sometimes, in the excitement of a conversation, we may forget to ask others about themselves and their thoughts, even when we are truly interested in them. And, as David learned, this can leave a different impression from what we intend.

Self-Check:

Do I end interactions knowing as much about the other person as they know about me?

Some Questions Are Better than Others David is a bit extreme. Most people know that a good way to show interest and get to know others is to ask questions. But not all questions are equal. The kinds of questions you ask and how you pose them will determine whether you end up making a deep connection or just skim the surface.

Let's compare a few approaches.

JUDY: What do you do?
FRED: I work for a nonprofit firm.
JUDY: Really, do you like it?
FRED: Yes, I do.
JUDY: How long have you been doing that?
FRED: Two years.

Judy showed interest in Fred, but because she used closed-ended questions, questions requiring only one-word responses, she missed the opportunity to get Fred to explain himself.

Let's imagine that the conversation went a different way.

JUDY: What do you do?
FRED: I work for a nonprofit firm.
JUDY: Really, that's cool. What kind of causes does your firm work with?
FRED: Well, all kinds of things. Right now I'm working on a project to understand health attitudes in Pacific Islanders. It's a great project for me.
JUDY: It is interesting. What do you like most about it?
FRED: Well, it makes me think about my own attitudes toward these things. Since I'm half Israeli, I've seen how culture can affect so many subtle aspects of life just from seeing the way my different grandparents approach things, like health and sports.

With closed-ended questions, you get what you ask for. In the second scenario, Judy's open-ended questions (like *"What kind of causes does your firm work with?" "What do you like most about it?"*) allowed Fred to open up about his work, and more.

Self-Check

Do I find myself exchanging surface information without getting to know people at a deeper level? Or do I ask open-
ended questions that solicit the other person's thoughts,
feelings, or interests?

A series of closed-ended questions can feel like an interrogation.
We've found that people who use this style of questioning have genuine curiosity, but present their inquiries in a rapid-fire way, with
mostly closed-ended questions. But the real hallmark of this approach
is the one-sidedness of the interchange. It's like never passing the
ball.

STEPHEN: Where do you live?
ELANA: Here in the city, on the Upper West Side.
STEPHEN: What street?
ELANA: Ninety-eighth.
STEPHEN: Do you like it uptown?
ELANA: Yes, it's—
STEPHEN: Where are you from originally?
ELANA: I grew up in New Jersey.
STEPHEN: Where exactly?
ELANA: In Montclair.
STEPHEN: What do you do?

Stephen bombarded Elana with so many questions that she had a
hard time catching her breath. She felt like she'd been taken in for
questioning.

Self-Check:

Do I let others take the lead or introduce topics? Do I ever notice myself interrupting others' responses with another question?

The Faux Segue Questions also can be used to circle the subject back to ourselves. The "faux segue" slyly moves the conversation to an area in which we can showcase an exceptional trait, knowledge, or experience.

Linda, an enthusiastic First Impressions client, gave a flawless example of the faux segue on her date. Linda asked "Nick" what he likes to do on the weekends. Nick explained that he is a runner and does most of his long runs on the weekends; he's actually preparing for a race. Linda nodded and then shared that she spends her Saturdays volunteering at a boys' club. She went on to say that she reads to kids who are having trouble at school and that it makes her feel great that she has helped so many kids.

Back at the office, here's how the feedback session went:

Linda's consultant pointed out that it was great that Linda shared what she enjoys and how she feels about it. But he also explained that before really responding to what he likes to do (i.e., running), she segued to a discussion about herself. Linda then admitted that she'd asked about Nick's weekends to create an opportunity for her to bring up her volunteer work, something that she is proud of. Her consultant helped Linda to see that while she did convey that she was a caring person, she also sent a few unintended messages, namely that she was not very interested in him and what he was doing and that she needed validation for her generosity.

An artful questioner uses open-ended questions that give others space to share their perspectives. Artful questions address feelings and opinions, not just facts, and follow up on others' responses to show real, not cursory, interest.

The Art of Listening

What you do after you ask a question can reveal even more about you than the questions you ask. You reveal your true level of interest in the way you listen.

Take the example of Matt, a well-groomed businessman with a precise demeanor, who was taking part in a leadership training workshop. He was looking forward to the workshop, but was also a little preoccupied with an important budget meeting he had later in the day and whether he would be able to make his daughter's dance recital as a result.

At Matt's first meeting with his workshop consultant, he began by greeting her and then asked a few polite questions about her background and experience. The consultant started to tell Matt about her previous projects for his company and mentioned that she knew one of Matt's colleagues. But before she had even finished her second sentence, she noticed that Matt had a glazed look on his face and his body seemed rigidly fixed in place. Matt's mind had drifted back to that budget meeting. The consultant sensed Matt's distraction and felt that he wasn't really interested in what she had to say. She was a little uncomfortable, so she hastily summarized her background and brought the conversation back to Matt by asking him about his current projects. That perked Matt back up. But she noticed that anytime she spoke, Matt assumed the look of a deflated balloon.

Live Listening Active listening is the difference between being fully present and genuinely attuned to someone's words and emotions and listening to a prerecorded telephone message while you check your e-mail. Sometimes, even with a live conversation, you may find yourself treating the other person like a recording and letting your mind drift. You may not always notice this, but others will. People are very sensitive to attention, and feel unappreciated and even frustrated when they sense that they are not listened to or understood.

LIKING YOUR OBSERVER

Even if people never say a word, you notice how they respond to you physically. And you probably make judgments about them and decide how much you like them based on their response.

Psychologists asked participants to speak about themselves for about five minutes on neutral topics, such as their hobbies and interests, while someone of the other sex watched and listened. The listeners were really confederates who varied how much they gazed, smiled, and leaned toward the participant as he or she spoke. The participant was then asked to evaluate the listener on a number of dimensions, including how likable he or she seemed.

Overall, male and female participants liked the silent listeners best when they gazed at them, smiled a lot, and leaned toward them.

So, in general, even if you never say anything, gazing, smiling, and leaning toward others will make them like you more than if you present a neutral body position.

Managing Mental Interruptions We've seen Matt's attention pattern in other clients: an ability to be present sporadically, especially when they speak, but withdrawing mentally when others speak. They may ask questions and go through the motions of showing interest, but then fail to listen actively. And they have no idea how their distraction is affecting their listener. It's difficult for most people to be totally attentive to others all the time. Distraction and mind wandering are natural and often involuntary.

You may not be able to prevent these mental distractions from occurring, but you can choose how you react to them. You can make an extra-special effort to attend to someone when meeting him or her for the first time. Inattentive listening, or "thinking away," is particula

noxious in a first impression. Even if you are generally very attentive, if you are distracted when you meet someone for the first time, the assumption will be that you do not find the person particularly intriguing or that you are a self-absorbed person in general.

Uh-huh   If you are actively listening to someone and want to show that you are, what can you do? There are some common ways to show attention: slowly saying "uh-huh," nodding, leaning toward them to catch every word, smiling or matching their emotion, and making good eye contact. These actions tell your listener that you are with them, that you are attentive and interested.

Faux Listening: Uh-huh, Uh-huh, Uh-huh   Just as there are faux segues—questions that are designed to move the focus back to the speaker—there is faux listening, also known as "waiting my turn to speak." That's when people feign that they are listening but are really just gathering their thoughts or waiting until they can break into the conversation. Faux listeners sometimes tip their hands. One way they do so is by showing the usual listening cues—but in a rapid manner. For example, if you say "Uh-huh, uh-huh, uh-huh" or nod your head rapidly when someone is speaking, it communicates impatience or a desire to turn the conversation back to yourself, rather than real interest.

William, who met Bob at their sons' basketball game, modeled the practice of faux listening. Here's how part of their conversation went:

BOB: I went skiing this weekend, the snow was great, but it was freezing! We had to go to the lodge a few times just to make sure we didn't get frostbitten.

WILLIAM (nodding): Uh-huh, uh-huh, uh-huh, yeah. . . .

BOB: I'd love to go again next weekend, but, man, don't know if it's worth it.

WILLIAM: Yeah, uh-huh. . . . Let me tell you about my weekend. . . . My son and I . . .

Bob then found himself listening to William's detailed story about his weekend escapades with his son. Every time Bob tried to take the floor, William nodded and "uh-huhed" impatiently until he could jump in. Bob finally excused himself from the conversation. He felt like he wasn't being listened to at all, and couldn't make a connection with William.

The Art of Responding

Now that you know how to pose questions and listen, what do you do when you are on the other side of the table? There is also an art to responding. Artful responses connect to the asker and aim to satisfy the asker's interest and expectations.

How Are You? Or, How Are You Really? One of our clients, Michael, told us about a conversation he had with a woman, Fiona, whom he met waiting for a train home after the Thanksgiving holiday. Michael is in his mid-30s, single, and has an easy manner about him. He was attracted to Fiona and wanted to get to know her. After discussing the train delay and the best place to buy a sandwich in the station, Michael asked Fiona how her holiday was. Fiona responded enthusiastically: "It was great! I went to my parents' house in Pennsylvania. I got there the night before, and I stayed up late with my brother and his kids playing Monopoly. The kids are about 10 and 12, no, maybe one is 13 now, I can't keep up, and maybe he is in fifth grade? Anyway, they weren't as good as we are, but we let the youngest one win. It was fun, though. Then on the holiday itself, I helped my mother roast a turkey on our outdoor grill. But it was really, really cold out, geez, it must have been 20 degrees! I had to keep running inside just to keep circulation in my fingers. And we had about 12 people for dinner, with, you know, the full spread...." She continued to tell Michael all the details of her weekend.

Fiona's response to Michael's question was more than he'd bargained for. *Way more.* Although interested at first, over time he began to feel inundated and annoyed. He had a hard time segueing to another topic and began looking for an excuse to escape the conversation.

Most of us understand that when someone asks, "How are you?" the question is meant as a pleasantry—especially with someone we've just met. We implicitly know that the questioner doesn't want a long-winded song and dance about how we *really* are, even if the person appears genuinely interested in us. But what kind of answer does someone expect to "How were your holidays?" It can be hard to judge. When in doubt, it's good to stay on the side of brevity. Michael would have been much more interested in Fiona if she had summarized the interesting elements of her holiday and responded briefly.

In general, the burden is on the person speaking to change the topic or turn the conversation toward the listener. In this example, it would have been awkward and difficult for Michael to have interrupted to change the topic or speak about himself without seeming rude or uninterested in Fiona.

Self-Check:

When asked a question, do I respond with my honest feelings and emotions, but *briefly*? Do I avoid excessive descriptions, and focus on the important and interesting information, so as not to bore or burden my listener?

That Reminds Me of Me   Good conversations are a fluid exchange of ideas and experiences. When we're listening to others, we naturally have associations about related experiences or stories. A back-and-forth sharing is the substance of connection. However, this interchange can be unbalanced if we frequently respond to others by relating topics back to ourselves. It's not a conscious desire to showcase our fine qualities (as in the faux segue) or a lack of listening, but rather an unedited, spontaneous response that shifts the focus to ourselves.

ALICIA: So, Nigel, how was your summer?

NIGEL: Not bad, I just got back from a vacation in the Southwest.

ALICIA: Really, I went to the Grand Canyon a few years ago. It was spectacular! A friend and I went on a ride to the bottom of the canyon on donkeys, and camped out, then we met some guides who told us...

Alicia fell into the "that reminds me of me" trap. She asked Nigel a question and listened; but Nigel reminded her of one of her own stories, which she couldn't resist sharing. While Alicia felt she was connecting to Nigel, she actually came across as uninterested and self-focused. Had she checked her urge to jump into her own story and first followed up to ask Nigel where he'd traveled and what he did, it would have sent only the positive message of interest.

Self-Check:

Do I give others the opportunity to finish their story or idea before adding any spontaneous associations I may have?

STYLE: YOUR INTEREST INTENSITY

The process of showing interest, as we just outlined, is about how you focus with your body and words, how you ask questions, listen, and respond. Separate from the process is your style—how intensely you show interest in others.

Are you aggressive, passive, or natural in the way you display your attention to others? Do you express interest lavishly, or do you try to play it cool? Your style probably depends on the situation and how comfortable you are with the other person. But you also may have a natural tendency to express your interest in a more open or closed manner.

MORE ABOUT ME:
CONVERSATIONAL NARCISSISM

Sometimes talking a lot about yourself can seem natural and feel good. But be careful. If you go too far, you can send people running for the door.

What makes a conversational narcissist? Psychologists have identified some key elements: boasting, refocusing the topic of the conversation on the self, speaking in a loud voice, using many "I" statements and inappropriately lengthy speech, and "glazing over" when others speak. Not surprisingly, conversational narcissism is a big turn-off. It violates the norm of reciprocity.

What do people do when coping with a conversational narcissist? Research shows that while some people try to change the topic, most people use a more passive response. They show a lack of interest and then look for a way to take their leave.

So if you find others disengaging and running to freshen their drink in the middle of one of your self-congratulatory stories, take note. You could be overdoing it. It may be a signal to change the topic to "somebody else."

Overdoing It: The One-Sided Approach

One of our First Impressions clients, Sam, is in his mid-20s and works as a pharmaceutical sales rep. He told us he meets lots of great women but was having trouble getting into a serious relationship. On his simulated date, he was very focused on Susan; he leaned toward her, smiled, and looked into her eyes. He opened the date by asking Susan the details of her day. He then asked her lots of questions about her hobbies, interests, and work. He sought her opinion on current events. He asked her what kind of movies and theater she liked. He listened attentively, asked follow-up questions, and related his comments to her ideas. He regularly used her name when making comments or asking questions. Susan was charmed by Sam's interest, energy, and focus on her. Sam wasn't directly complimenting her, but his attention alone made her feel understood and attractive. However, in the course of the date, Susan realized that Sam asked a lot about her but shared little of himself. In fact, he allowed her little opportunity to ask about him. The conversation was very one-sided.

Sam showered Susan with attention and interest. While it had an overall positive effect, it did raise some flags in Susan's mind. She wondered whether Sam was a private person and not open to connection. She also questioned what his motive was in showering her with such attention and thought that he might always be this way when first meeting people, thereby depersonalizing his display of interest. When she brought this up in the feedback session, Sam explained that he always tries to draw women out on first dates and even plans in advance certain questions to ask. But he didn't know that this style made him appear private or not genuine. He didn't realize that his attention and constant questioning were, in effect, controlling the conversation and limiting her opportunities to reciprocate interest in him.

To Compliment or Not to Compliment

Many of our clients wonder about whether and how they should compliment others in social or business situations. Will it win others over, or send the wrong message? In general, it's a good thing to do, and will make a good impression. Receiving a compliment makes people feel appreciated and respected, and usually results in greater liking for the complimenter.

However, focus matters. Of all the qualities to compliment someone on during a first meeting, the safest is personal accomplishments or talents. We've noted that our clients generally feel proud of their accomplishments and are comfortable talking about them. Style and taste are good too. We've found people are more comfortable responding to compliments about their clothing or style, which reflects a personal choice, than compliments about their body, which they may have sensitivities about.

FLATTERY WILL GET YOU FAR

Usually it is obvious when someone is trying to ingratiate himself with another person. But what about when we are the targets of flattery? How does that make us feel toward the person doing the flattering?

Researchers have posed these questions. In one study, participants were asked to read flattering descriptions either about themselves or about another person. The description was supposedly written by a "stranger" (other study participants whom they did not know) based on information the stranger had received about them. In reality, all participants received the same very positive description, unrelated to any personal information about them.

The findings showed that when the flattery was about themselves versus someone else, the participants more strongly liked the stranger, and their mood was enhanced. This was true regardless of the motives ascribed to the stranger and regardless of whether the stranger's description matched the participant's own self-description. In addition, if participants thought that they would be interacting with the stranger in the future, they liked the person even more.

The flattered participants did not consider the stranger to be insincere. This phenomenon may exist because most psychologically healthy people think highly of themselves and believe that they are above average in most qualities. Flattery is thus consistent with this self-image; it makes sense and is easy to believe.

The researchers concluded that "people like those who flatter them and tend to believe in their sincerity in spite of strong situational cues indicating otherwise."

Delivery matters too. Some people don't like receiving a compliment in the form of a direct statement, as in "You have a great body," because it forces a reaction. The complimented person usually has two choices: to politely thank or to awkwardly deny, as in "Well, my hips are really big, I don't like them." However, compliments delivered in a way that furthers the flow of the conversation are comfortable for most people and provide an avenue for further engagement in the interaction. For example, "That's great that you practice yoga, it seems so good for you." In this case, the complimenter offers his companion an opportunity to share more about this personal interest in a way that continues, rather than interrupts, the flow of conversation.

"SUCKING UP" AT WORK

There are lots of ways to curry favor at work. These include flattery, modesty (such as apologizing), doing favors, agreeing with others' opinions, and self-promoting. Researchers have examined the effectiveness of these techniques on subordinates, peers, and superiors.

Overall, the findings show that all of these techniques do work, at least to some degree. People who use them are liked more and get better evaluations. The techniques worked with everyone, but worked better on subordinates and peers than on superiors. With superiors, the most successful technique was flattery and the least successful was self-promotion. When the ingratiation becomes more obvious, and it's clear that the ingratiator has an agenda, the effect is lessened.

So you may be liked more and evaluated better if you ingratiate yourself at work. Just beware that actively promoting yourself and showing an obvious desire to impress may backfire. Especially if it's to your boss. Remember, moderation is key.

Underplaying It: Undisclosed Interest

Sam, the very interested pharmaceutical sales rep described earlier, is an unusual First Impressions client. Many of our clients have the opposite style—they are skittish about displaying interest. They tend to not focus on others very strongly, to not ask many questions, and are hesitant about verbalizing any attraction or interest. Rather, they talk about themselves and objective topics, such as current events and culture. They don't show a lot of interest because they don't want to appear needy or inferior, or be vulnerable to rejection. Sometimes they are intimidated by someone's strengths and don't want to ask more about them or acknowledge them because it reinforces their own feelings of inferiority. For many, it's just a habit. On a first meeting, they just don't express a lot of interest in others, even when they are genuinely curious.

However, while this approach may feel "safe," it has some real drawbacks. That's because there is a huge reciprocity in interest. If you show people that you are interested in them, like them, and respect them, they are simply more likely to feel the same way about you than if they don't know your feelings of interest or attraction. *Thus, if you show interest in someone, you are more likely to be the object of his or her interest.*

Self-Check:

Am I comfortable expressing genuine interest and respect for someone I've just met, even if I feel inferior to the person in some way?

The Third Way: Confident Interest

Take another one of our First Impressions clients, Amy, a young schoolteacher from the Bronx who met her simulated date in a museum café. Here's how part of her simulated date went:

AMY: So, Nick, what do you like to do for fun?

NICK: Well, I play around with video as a hobby. I've made a couple of films with friends and family, just for fun, nothing serious.

AMY: That's really impressive. I don't know anyone who's actually made a movie, although lots of people I know have video cameras. How did you decide to do that?

NICK: Hmm, I'm not really sure exactly. But I have some friends in theater, and I think they may have planted the idea.

AMY: You seem like a creative guy. That's cool. I would like to be more creative. I have a little talent in music, but I haven't really explored it.

Nick felt appreciated for his creative accomplishment. Amy showed sincere interest and complimented Nick in a way that made him comfortable opening up to her and telling her more about himself. How Amy responded to him also created a way for him to convey his interest in her. They went on to have a lively conversation about a wide variety of topics and connected easily.

Like Amy, you have a lot to gain by expressing genuine interest in others. It makes people feel appreciated, appealing, and understood. All these benefits make the other person more open to connecting with you. As long as it is done in a way that is sincere, furthers the conversation, and does not minimize your self-expression, it is likely to make a good first impression. By showing her interest so readily, Amy appeared self-confident and comfortable with herself, which made her all the more appealing to Nick.

SUMMARY

Interest is a gift you can give someone. Most people want to be understood and will appreciate your attention and focus. When you meet people for the first time, you know very little about them besides what is visible, and you may make quick assumptions that may or may not reflect their real self. Demonstrating an interest in learning about them and an appreciation for who they are will likely result in a reciprocal interest and build a foundation of connection.

The process of showing your interest involves directing your physical energy toward others—looking, leaning, and nonverbally responding to them. It also consists of asking questions, listening closely, and responding appropriately. You show your interest style in the intensity of your curiosity and how you compliment or show your appreciation for others.

As you read through the following tables, think about how you show your interest in others during a first conversation. Are you aware of how you express your attention and interest? Are you demonstrative or shy? What kind of interest do you show? Again, think about each behavior and check off whether you do it usually, sometimes, or rarely.

POSITIVE INTEREST BEHAVIORS

If You Do This:	You May Seem:	Do I Do This?		
		Usually	Sometimes	Rarely
Lean toward others when they are speaking	Interested, attracted, affirming			
Make eye contact	Interested, socially aware			
Use the other's name in the conversation	Focused, connected, attentive			
Ask questions of your conversational partner	Interested, attracted			
Listen actively	Not self-absorbed, engaged, focused			
Compliment or genuinely express your respect for someone	Affirming, understanding, likable			

COMMON MISCOMMUNICATIONS

If You Do This:	You May Think You Seem:	But You May Seem:	Do I Do This?		
			Usually	Sometimes	Rarely
Listen inactively	Neutral	Uninterested, rejecting, preoccupied			
Talk about yourself without asking about the other person	Informative, interesting	Self-absorbed, rude, tedious			
Hold the floor by asking many questions	Interested, attracted	Private, controlling			
Use questions to segue the focus back to yourself	Interested, connecting	Self-absorbed, uninteresting			
Withhold attention or interest	Cool and confident	Uninterested, rejecting, cold			

Pass the Topic: The Subject
Matter of First Conversations

Now you know the first two fundamentals of first impressions: how to invite others to you and show interest in them. Then what? As you engage in a dialogue with someone, you have the opportunity to create an interesting—rather than humdrum—conversation. How do you do that? You demonstrate the third first impression fundamental when you generate and explore topics from the world around you—about life, current events, culture, and your observations thereof.

When you talk about the world around you, you provide the social gift of enlightenment. You satisfy others' interest in new ideas and perspectives. And it shows good qualities in *you*. When you share and discuss topics about the world, you seem curious and engaged in life. If you show little awareness or interest in life and ideas around you, you may seem boring, self-absorbed, or both.

But even the worldly and well informed can get tripped up in a first conversation. We've all been in situations where we're a little tongue-tied and have thought, "What am I going to talk about with this person? Should I talk about the weather, my model airplane hobby, the price of gasoline, or my position on gun control?" Of course it's easy to pick topics with friends; you know each other's interests and probably share many of them. With new people, you are mutual blank slates. The only way to get acquainted is to cross that line and explore some topics.

In this chapter we focus on how you discuss objective topics—topics about the world around you. This reflects your *intellectual* self-presentation. It demonstrates how you process information—how analytical, creative, and open-minded you are. In contrast, how you discuss subjective topics—personal information and feelings—reflects your *emotional* self-presentation. We'll talk about that in Chapter 7 on self-disclosure.

Here we explore the process, style, and content of your intellectual self-presentation. The process is the order and manner in which you introduce and navigate topics, your style is whether you are interactive or one-sided, and content is the actual topics you bring up. We'll show you that how you talk about topics matters more than what you actually talk about. You can make a fascinating ethical issue boring if you simply lecture someone about it. On the other hand, you can turn your model airplane hobby into a stimulating conversational topic if you talk about it in a fun and engaging manner.

PROCESS: THE LOGISTICS OF DISCUSSION

We'll start with the logistics. That's the order in which you bring up subjects of discussion, the ways you generate and respond to topics, and how you check for others' interest in the topics you bring up.

The Usual Order

Even though a first conversation feels new and unique, there are norms about the way discussions open up. In fact, there is a very common and ritualistic sequence of discussing objective topics with someone you've just met. We usually start with the "field," move to "facts," and ease into the "fun stuff." If you follow this sequence, you'll likely make others feel more comfortable about you. And it can make a conversation easier to navigate if you are at a loss on how to get started.

Level 1. The Field: Where We Are

Initial topics are usually about the current environment or situation—how you got there, the weather, or the location—as discussed in Chapter 4 on accessibility. It's almost obligatory to mention something about the current place or time. Then we typically explore whether we have mutual friends or other connections. Engaging in this ritual helps others to connect you to their world and to feel relaxed around you.

Level 2. The Facts: What's Happening

What do you talk about after you've talked about the weather? There is a critical, and sometimes awkward, moment after you've finished discussing the rain, when someone has to make a "topic initiative." Some first conversations can feel like a fishing expedition—you throw a topic out and see if your conversational partner bites. And we usually start with facts: "Did you hear about...?" There is good reason for doing so. Facts are safe. There's little risk of offending anyone or causing conflict.

Level 3. The Fun Stuff: Ideas and Opinions

While safe, facts aren't usually as fun as ideas. Attitudes, ideas, and opinions are much more savory fare. It's from discussions at this level that people often decide whether they connect with someone and whether they'd like to develop a friendship. However, ideas and opinions are riskier than facts. Going into the "idea space" runs the risk of uncovering differences of values. That's why people typically warm up with pleasantries and facts and then ease into ideas.

ATTITUDES OF ATTRACTION

What makes someone attracted to you? Psychologists have explored many factors, including physical qualities, cooperativeness, and intelligence, among others. One strong finding is that people are attracted to you if you share the same attitudes about life—such as parenting, welfare legislation, smoking, and foreign movies.

Why is that? For starters, it's validating. It affirms a person's ability to be sensible, interpret the world correctly, and make good predictions about the future. Another reason is that people naturally assume that those who share their attitudes will like them. So if you agree with someone about the death penalty, he assumes you will like him more than if you didn't agree. Because he assumes you like him, he likes you.

If you want to be favorably received, show others where you have similar attitudes. See if you can find where you agree rather than disagree. Remember, everyone prefers to hear "you're right" rather than "you're wrong."

Situation Variation

Of course, not every first conversation follows this order, and some situations specifically allow you to quickly jump into "Level 3" topics—the fun stuff. For example, when you are at a meeting organized around a common interest, like a community board meeting, a computer show, a road runners' group, you tend to jump right to Level 3. In these situations, you already know that you have interests in common. You may start talking about the common theme—for example, new zoning laws or training routines, and your opinions on them—and skip the warm-up steps. If you want to get to know someone better in these situations, you may have to "work backward" and discuss the location or current events and share personal information.

Casting a Line: Generating Topics

Regardless of the situation, it's preferable to bring up *some* topic in a first conversation rather than none at all. Consider one of our First Impressions clients, Lenny, who met his consultant for a simulated date late one winter afternoon. Here's how part of the conversation went:

SUSAN: So, Lenny, are you planning to watch the Oscars next week?
LENNY: No, I don't go to the movies very often.
SUSAN: Yeah, I haven't seen that many either, but I still like to see who wins and see what they wear.
LENNY (nodding): Yeah, I know a lot of people will be watching.
(Pause)
SUSAN: Oh, did you read the Sunday paper? Apparently there's a polar ice cap that's melted! I guess this global warming thing is for real.
LENNY: Really, what's happening with it?

Susan went on to explain what she read, and Lenny commented, until she introduced another topic. This pattern went on for an hour.

In the feedback session, Lenny said that he enjoyed the conversation and thought that he came across as attentive and engaged. He said he especially likes to be around people like Susan who are interested in things he doesn't follow. His consultant explained that although he seemed to be attentive and interested, she felt burdened with carrying the conversation and frustrated by his lack of contribution. She felt denied the opportunity to be informed or entertained by Lenny.

In general, if you don't add any ideas or topics to the conversation, you may be perceived as dull, even though you may have acted attentive and felt engaged.

Getting Stuck
Here's the experience of our friend Jack, a man in his early 30s who had recently moved to New York City from Miami. Jack's boss invited

> ## A RECIPE FOR BOREDOM
>
> There are many ways to be a bore, unfortunately.
>
> Researchers have studied boredom in interpersonal inter-actions by asking people to listen to conversations and rate them on a number of dimensions.
>
> The findings show that people who are passive and add very little objective information to a conversation are seen as more boring than those who contribute more, no matter what the content is. These low-contributing, passive communica-tors are judged to be more socially insecure and are liked less than the more active contributors.
>
> Responding to others' topics and having a topic or two to introduce goes a long way. It's enlightening and entertaining to your conversational partner, and it presents you in a posi-tive light.

him to a dinner party at his house. Jack was hoping to meet some new people and dressed up in order to make a good impression. At the dinner, Jack was seated next to Vanessa, his boss's neighbor, a quiet woman about Jack's age. Jack and Vanessa introduced themselves, asked each other what they did, where they lived, and how they knew the host. Then there was an awkward silence. Jack asked Vanessa how she liked the meal. She said it was delicious; she particularly liked the fish. Another silence. Vanessa then asked Jack how he liked the res-taurants in New York. Jack said he'd only had an opportunity to try a few and that they were definitely better than the ones in Miami. Vanessa agreed. After a few more exchanges about places to buy fish, Jack and Vanessa found themselves frantically looking back to the group, hoping to be brought into another conversation.

Obviously, Jack and Vanessa had some trouble generating a topic "with legs." They were stuck in Level 1, The Field. They covered the situation, their connection, and the food. But they never got to Level 2,

The Facts, and embarked on a topic, let alone shared any Level 3 topics, The Fun Stuff. The scene was set, but they failed to get to the next act.

You probably know people who are always full of exciting news and information. These topic-generators usually are stimulating and engaging to be around. How do they do it? They seem to have lots of juicy topics at their fingertips. Some of the topics may come from things they have seen on TV, read, or been told about. But many of their interesting topics may be their own observations and commentary on everyday life. They are skilled in gleaning ideas that may be interesting to others and adapting their subject matter to their conversational partners.

Getting Out of a Jam
If you're at a loss for topics, you can always ask a question: "Did you hear about...?" "What do you think about...?" Either Jack or Vanessa could have taken their conversation to another level by throwing out more questions, especially about Level 2 and 3 topics—facts and opinions. For example, Jack could have added, "I'm new to the city and haven't followed the local politics. What do you think of the mayor's latest plan to...?" Or Vanessa could have asked, "What was it like in Miami, what's happening there?"

Self-Check:

Am I able to move a conversation beyond the warm-up stage by generating topics of discussion? Do I have a sense of what topics may be interesting to others? Can I charge up a conversation when needed?

Taking a Bite: Responding to Topics

Of course, part of conversing is responding to topics that others generate. It's great when the topic is something you know about and share an interest in. If someone asks you about your favorite sports team or musician, you usually can come up with thoughts and opinions.

Topics You Don't Know

But there are lots of topics you don't know anything about. That's part of the fun of meeting someone new—learning new things and seeing new perspectives. Yet sometimes when someone introduces an alien topic, you fear looking ignorant, and change or ignore the topic. Unfortunately, in such cases you actually may come across as rude, self-absorbed, or socially awkward.

Here's part of an interaction between Rob and George, unacquainted coworkers who chatted at the office coffee machine one Monday morning.

ROB: Well, it's been quite a weekend at my house. With both my sons having soccer practice and my wife's family in town, I'm wiped out! I wish I had more time to chill.

GEORGE: I know what you mean. But I was sick this weekend so I had some time to lie around and watch TV. Just last night I saw this documentary on Lincoln. It was really well done. I never knew that—

ROB: Really . . . I missed that one. . . . I'm more into music myself. I was watching a video on the golden age of jazz. I really like that kind of music.

Rob, who knows very little about history, was feeling uncomfortably ignorant when George talked about the documentary and was embarrassed to expose himself by following up on the topic. So he changed the topic. However, George found Rob to be awkward, uninterested, and rude. Rob's behavior was the opposite of the faux segue—where someone strategically moves the topic toward something he'd like to show off. Rob strategically moved the conversation *away* from a topic he'd like to avoid.

You don't have to be knowledgeable on a broad range of topics to make a positive first impression. All you have to do is show curiosity about others' areas of interest or opinions. Most people are not at all put off by others' unfamiliarity; in fact, they may relish the opportunity to tell you about a favorite topic. For example, Rob could have said, "I don't know much about Lincoln at all; what was the documentary about?" and come across much more positively. If you change the topic out of fear of showing your ignorance, people may register your behavior as lack of interest in their favorite subject and see you less positively than if you were genuine about your lack of knowledge.

Self-Check:

How do I respond when others bring up topics of which I have no knowledge? Do I try to learn from them, or do I try to maneuver to a topic in which I have more confidence?

Topics You Know Yet Don't Love

Sometimes, however, you meet a new person who brings up a topic that you know something about but aren't interested in. It's particularly challenging when someone carries on about that subject at length. Here's an experience of our client Hanna's, who was seated next to Ray on a flight from Boston to Dallas one evening. During the beverage service, Ray introduced himself and struck up a conversation with Hanna.

RAY: Hi, I'm Ray. Do you live in Dallas?
HANNA: No, I'm from Boston myself, and you?
RAY: I was in Boston for a conference. It's an annual event, and it was really interesting this year. I'm in the laundry equipment business. Do you know anything about it?

TOPIC TOOLS

Although you may not notice it, there is a common format for discussing topics. Someone throws a topic on the table, and somehow it gets discussed. How does that work?

Researchers have found that there is a common manner of managing a topic. It doesn't always follow the same exact order, but some of the elements are questions, discussing behavior, and getting and discussing facts. For example, if you are talking about sports, you might ask "Did you see the Mets game last night?" then move on to "I can't believe they pulled the pitcher in the fourth inning." And then to "What do you know about their new pitcher? I heard he had an injury." Then you may move on to another topic, such as travel or politics, and the whole process begins anew: a little Q and A, talk about behavior, and sharing and discussing facts. And so on with the next topic.

This topic management gets repeated over and over, like cycles within a conversation. It's a helpful tool. It's especially handy when you encounter a topic you know nothing about. For example, if someone throws out the topic of Oriental carpets, and you know nothing about them, start with some questions: "Are they still making them the same way as they did centuries ago?" and so on. It gives you conversational flexibility and fluidity.

HANNA: No, actually, not much.
RAY: Most people don't know it, but there is tremendous innovation in the industry. I work for a relatively new company, Smart Wash—have you heard of it?
HANNA: Smart Wash? I don't think so.
RAY: Well, what kind of machine do you have?

HANNA: You know, I'm not sure; it came with the house when we bought it last year. I think it's a Maytag.

RAY: Well, Maytags are great machines, but Smart Wash is the leader in fabric softener delivery and timing. This feature alone makes a huge difference in how fabrics feel after laundering; it's like night and day with towel texture. Are you particular about your fabrics? What's your favorite?

HANNA (looking across the aisle to see if there are any other seats available, and then back to Ray): You know, I never thought about it, but I can imagine that would be important. Me, I'm into convenience. I like to send my laundry out.

Ray was actually trying to engage Hanna in his favorite topic. He wanted an interaction. But after a few minutes talking laundry, and just before the dinner cart was wheeled down the aisle, Hanna excused herself and said she had some work to do. She grabbed her bag and found a seat a few rows back.

Hanna was not impressed with her seatmate. Because of his focus on a topic she was not interested in, she found Ray to be a boring companion. Now, it could be that Ray is uncomfortable with new people and sticks with topics he is confident in while he may actually have broad interests. But Hanna never found that out. And Hanna most likely did not make a great first impression on Ray, especially after her abrupt exit.

Hanna didn't seem to care what impression Ray had of her. But assuming she wanted to make a positive impression because they knew people in common, or was just in the mood for a pleasant conversation, what could she have done differently? It may have been challenging, but if she tried to steer the conversation to another topic, they both may have had a more enjoyable experience. Often we feel it would be impolite to change the subject when we are uninterested, but we may actually be doing ourselves and our conversational partners a favor. We are relieved of boredom, and they get the chance to learn about something new and connect with us. Most people would like that opportunity but may not know how to get there. Most would generally prefer it to an outright rejection.

Let's imagine the interaction went a little differently:

RAY: ... This feature alone makes a huge difference in how fabrics feel after laundering; it's like night and day with towel texture.

HANNA: Wow, sounds like you really know a lot about laundry! Me? I confess I don't spend much time on it. I like to go out a lot, I'm actually a film buff, I see as many movies as I can. Have you seen...?

While there is no guarantee that Ray would be interested in film, he may have realized that he was limiting the subject of the discussion. And he may have made an effort to hear about Hanna's interests. Hanna certainly had little to lose. Changing the topic abruptly out of discomfort, as Rob did in the previous example, may not be appealing. However, changing the topic after hearing someone out can be an act of social generosity.

Self-Check:

When I am uninterested in a topic, do I surrender to boredom, escape the scene, or take the initiative to change the topic?

Yawn

Sometimes, if you're really into something, you might "pull a Ray" and talk more than another person's interests accommodate. That's why it's good form in first conversations to limit discussions of your favorite topics and check for cues from others.

The best cues are in your conversation partner's body language. If she is looking away, disengaged, or withdrawn, chances are she's growing bored and impatient. If you notice this happening, you can use it as a signal to change the subject or ask a question. Ray, for example, failed to respond to Hanna's body language when she looked away from him. These boredom behaviors are rarely faked—they generally reflect people's real emotions. If they are faked at all, they are usually exaggerated to signal a lack of interest to the speaker.

Nodding, eye contact, smiling, and leaning in, on the other hand, are indicators of interest. If you see these signs, you can assume that others share your enthusiasm. However, beware of body language deception. Most people, at least from time to time, fake interest. They're polite, and smile and nod, even though they're thinking that they can't wait to escape the conversation.

Checking and Ending

If you want to look for sincere interest, you have at least two options. You could check for interest in your topic, or close the topic and see if your listener asks for more information. To check, you can solicit a little feedback about others' engagement before diving deeper—as in "If you are really interested, I could tell you more of the details." This is good form. But beware: People may find it hard to tell you on a first meeting that they, in fact, are not interested. So they may "verbally deceive" and say, "Yeah, sure, I'm interested..." in order to be polite.

The better option is to be brief, give the broad strokes, and then close the topic. For example, Ray could have briefly described his conference and then closed with "Anyway, Boston was great. Fun city!" This way Hanna would be free to either change the topic or, if interested, ask Ray follow-up questions—without any fear of being impolite. Ray also could have turned the conversation back to Hanna more directly. He could have asked her a question, such as "So what do you do in Boston?" Remember, the burden is on the speaker to turn the conversation to the other.

Self-Check:

When talking about a topic I'm excited about, am I careful to be brief and then turn the conversation to the other? Do I give others the social freedom to either introduce a new topic or follow up on something I'm talking about?

YOUR TOPICS STYLE

So far we've addressed how you discuss topics. Now we'll turn our attention to the style in which you discuss information. Style is about how interactive or one-sided you are and how open- or closed-minded you appear. For instance, do you present information as "I learned something that was interesting..." or "I've got it all figured out, and I'm going to tell you"?

The Engaging Style—"Talking With"

An attractive way to discuss topics is to be interactive: You throw some subjects on the table and respond to topics others bring up. It's an equal exchange. No one person plays "entertainer" and no one plays "audience." When you "talk with," you appear interested in the world and in others' perspectives, as well as socially skilled and comfortable with yourself.

This may sound simple, but many people stray from this style—especially if they are feeling nervous during a first meeting. The most common violation of "talking with" is "talking at"—forcing others to react rather than interact.

Demanding an Audience—"Talking At"

Talking about what interests you is a normal part of your interactions with family and friends. You may come home to your spouse and say,

SECRETS OF SKILLED CONVERSATIONALISTS

As you've surely noticed, some people are more skilled in making conversation with strangers than others. Why is that? What do they know or do that makes them so good at it?

Researchers have identified two key elements of a successful conversational style. One element is being proactive and thinking about a goal for the interaction, as in "I wanted to make her comfortable, so I talked about her interests." The second element is being reactive. Skilled conversationalists are acutely sensitive to the situation and others' styles, and adapt themselves, as in "The person seemed shy, so I decided to talk about myself a bit." Depending on whom they are speaking to, they can be talkative or quiet, fast or slow, and so on.

We can all learn from the secrets of these successful conversationalists. We can pay attention to our conversational goal and adapt to others and the situation.

"Oh, I have to tell you what I heard today..." or "I think I've figured out..." and explain at length some story or thought.

However, the same behavior generally does not play out so well with strangers. That's because first encounters are relatively short, and when you are in "tell" mode, you force others into "react" mode. When people are pushed into an audience mode in their first conversation with you, they may experience it as a waste of their time, a burden, or a denial of the opportunity to interact. Being talked at can be enormously boring and a real kiss of death in a first impression.

Talking a lot isn't always talking at. For example, Ray in the last example talked a lot, but he was actually trying to engage his seatmate, Hanna. He asked her questions—about her washing machine, of course, and where she was from, and her favorite fabric. Talking at is a special category of talking a lot. The hallmark of the "at" approach is that roles are defined. Someone assumes the role of the teller; the other, often by no choice of her own, plays the audience.

There are four ways to "talk at." One form is lecturing—presenting facts or your synthesis of them. Another form is telling extended stories about people or events. A third way is sermonizing—that is, trying to convince others of your way of thinking. And a fourth way is telling jokes—dominating a conversation with jokes and wit in a way that positions your listener as an audience.

"Talking at" Style 1: The Lecture Circuit

Sometimes, out of a sincere desire to share interesting information, we may find ourselves presenting a lecture or a "data dump" on others. While you may think you never do that, we've seen that many people can fall into the lecture trap at least occasionally.

Take one of our clients, Jason, a successful manager in a large technology company. Jason told his consultant about a devastating experience that happened early in his career when he was a 25-year-old sales rep. One day Jason was at a lunch with new clients from a financial services company. After brief small talk, Martin, the CFO, mentioned that he was recovering from a back injury and lamented about his experience with the medical industry. Jason, who was very interested in politics and policy, knew a lot about health care. So he started speaking about "the problem with health care in America," including a summary of the various positions on the industry, from the origins of the modern health system, to the Clinton administration initiatives, to the present situation. Martin and the others sat politely and listened, until finally the waiter interrupted to take their coffee order.

Lecturing is always a positive experience for the lecturer. Jason felt great and, blinded by his own self-satisfaction, thought everyone else did too. Further, he felt he came across as smart and informed. The clients, however, had a different impression, as Jason later found out. They thought Jason was bright, but also pompous and boring. Following that lunch, they called Jason's manager and explained their reaction. They asked to be assigned to another sales rep.

Male-Pattern Lecturing Men, we've found, tend to lecture more than women do. And men tend to lecture to women more than they do to other men. Some lecturing males project an I've-got-it-all-figured-out attitude. When we question our male clients about their behavior, they say that they feel good knowing that they've informed someone about something meaningful. These men are consistently unaware of the fact that they often turn their conversational partners into conversational victims—trapping them into a listening, reactive mode.

A hallmark of a lecture is the speaker's implicit ownership of the information. Jason didn't reference where he learned the information or how he formed his ideas. He presented the information as "his" treatise on "the problem with health care," not an opinion he formed from reading particular op-ed articles or other sources. When you present something as your own, you may intend to appear smart but actually may appear bombastic and egotistical. On the other hand, when you mention where you learned your information—as in "I read an editorial in the paper that said . . ."—or the genesis of your idea—as in "I saw something on TV, and then thought . . ."—you show an open mind and a more modest assessment of your own intellectual value.

"Talking at" Style 2: Storytelling

Telling stories is another form of talking at. But instead of focusing on facts and analyses, it's relaying of stories, events, and the experiences of others we know. Stories are often the stuff of human interaction. They're a great way to entertain and connect with others. However, storytelling can be a form of "talking at" if the stories are long, detailed, and about people your conversational partner doesn't know. Like a lecture, storytelling fails to engage the listener and demands an audience.

Remember Michael and Fiona at the train station? Fiona fell into storytelling when she relayed a long and detailed description of her family's Thanksgiving. Here's another example. Scott and Samantha are 50-something suburbanites who met at the barbecue of a mutual friend. They struck up a conversation while sipping lemonade and milling around the grill.

Here's how part of the conversation went:

SCOTT: Hi, you look familiar. I think I might have seen you at Ted and Abby's last barbecue. Ted and I are old friends from school. I'm Scott.

SAMANTHA: Hi, I'm Samantha. We live two doors down, you can see our backyard, it's the green house. It's feeling big. My husband and I will be empty nesters next year. My youngest daughter, Julie, is going to college.

SCOTT: Oh, that's exciting for her.

SAMANTHA: Yes, she's thinking of majoring in economics. Which I think is great. But Julie isn't sure where she wants to go. She's thinking that she'd prefer a small school; she's sort of quiet and thinks she might get lost in a crowd. My nephew went to UCLA, but she doesn't think she'd be comfortable there. . . .

SCOTT (looking around): Well, it's an important decision.

Samantha went on to describe in detail all of her daughter's college options and extracurricular activities, until Scott excused himself.

Scott had never met Samantha's daughter and was not terribly interested in hearing about her in such detail. Samantha, however, was very absorbed in her daughter's college decision and was unaware that in telling this story, she was forcing Scott to be her audience and was coming across as boring and banal.

As a general rule, on a first meeting, you'll connect to others better if you keep your stories short and to the point.

"Talking at" Style 3: Sermonizing

The third category of "talking at" is sermonizing—trying to convince someone of your way of thinking. It's expounding on your politics, values, views, religion, philosophy, or an issue you feel passionately about. Such topics may be an important part of your life and great subject matter for conversations with those close to you. However, presenting rigid opinions usually does not play well on first impressions.

Take the example of Nathan, one of our First Impressions clients. Here's how part of his conversation went:

NATHAN: What's your favorite book?

SUSAN: Oh, I don't know, I guess I'm partial to books I read as a teenager, like *Sense and Sensibility*. I always loved that one. Do you have a favorite?

NATHAN: Yes, *The Fountainhead* by Ayn Rand. Do you know it?

SUSAN: I know of it, but I've never read it.

NATHAN: It's great, really, Rand is a great writer. She has a political theory, but also writes about art and aesthetics as well. She feels that art represents man's fundamental views of himself and his existence. For example, take the Empire State Building—it's actually a virtue because it's the union of art and practical needs.

SUSAN: Hmm. I love the Empire State Building. But I never thought of it as a "virtue." But I like the German Expressionists' influence...

Nathan strongly disagreed. He went on to explain more of Ayn Rand's work and philosophy to Susan and tried to convince her of Rand's interpretation of art. Susan was interested at first, but then began to feel the conversation became less of an exchange and more of a sermon.

The hallmark of a sermon is that it is delivered with the intention of convincing or converting someone. The implicit message is "you're wrong and I'm right." The preacher is informing his listener, but with an agenda of pushing his own framework, values, politics, or religion.

Now, Nathan was an extreme example, but most of us have some ideas, perspectives, or politics that we may try to sell to others, *maybe just a little bit*. It could be a favorite issue, such as animal rights or SUV safety, that you like to bring up with the agenda of expressing your views. However, others have their own views of the world and, in general, prefer to be with people who affirm those views, not challenge them. While you don't have to hide your values, you may want to think about which are critical to you and whether they are important enough to introduce at a first meeting. Remember, you generally make a better impression if you first focus on understanding the other person's values and avoid trying to convert her to your way of thinking.

Do I sometimes attempt to convince people I've just met on the merits of my life philosophy, values, religion, or politics? Am I ever dogmatic about an issue?

Curbing Your Convictions You can discuss almost any topic, even topics on which you have strong opinions, with a stranger and make a positive first impression if you show interest in other perspectives and a sincere desire to understand other ways of thinking. Even if you have very strong political beliefs, for instance, you can still discuss politics as long as you also show genuine interest in the other person's opinion. A measure of success in this effort is to leave an interaction having learned something about a different perspective, rather than feeling frustrated for failing to influence someone.

Self-Check:

Do I walk away from interactions with new people having learned something new on a topic that I have strong opinions on?

"Talking at" Style 4: Telling Jokes

Humor and levity are charming qualities to bring to any first conversation. They elevate others' moods, relax people, and foster connection. In short, they are good things. However, telling jokes doesn't come across well when it's done in a one-way manner, such that the jokester is "talking at" the listener, who is forced into a reactionary or audience role.

Take Greg, an affable man in his early 30s. He accompanied a friend to a holiday party and met two attractive women in whom he took an immediate interest. He wanted to entertain them and appear witty. So, after some opening pleasantries, Greg launched into some of his favorite jokes. The women were genuinely charmed at first, laughed at the jokes, and enjoyed his company. However, as Greg continued, they found themselves assuming the role of an audience and felt obliged to keep laughing at Greg's jokes. Of course, some weren't as funny as others, but to be polite, they feigned amusement. Even after Greg turned the conversation to them and asked questions, he repeatedly injected humor into his responses, again forcing a reaction from his new acquaintances. The women were soon bored with the audience role and moved on, somewhat abruptly, to strike up a conversation with another guest, leaving Greg perplexed. He thought he was being funny and entertaining.

Greg actually *was* being funny. But his sense of humor turned the corner from connecting to alienating when he assumed the role of "performer" and forced an audience. He may have made a much better impression if he told only a few jokes and moved on to other ways of connecting. That way he wouldn't have demanded reactions. Also, jokes carry some risk with new people. As you've surely noted, jokes can be idiosyncratic in their appeal and ability to offend. What one person finds hilarious, someone else finds ho-hum or sexist.

CONTENT: CONVERSATIONAL FODDER

Now that we've covered the process and style of discussing objective topics, we turn our attention to the actual content. Our clients often ask us specifically what they should talk about with new people. The answer is almost any topic—if you present it in a comfortable and engaging manner. But remember to ease from the mild to the strong, as we discussed in the beginning of the chapter.

While there are few topics that are totally off limits if you find common ground with someone and have mutual interest, there are some guidelines on what makes for more comfortable fare.

The Simple and the Relevant

Some topics are appealing simply because they are standard in first meetings. The immediate situation—such as the weather and the place—is the start. Then people usually move on to talk about the surrounding world—such as current events, public interest stories, sports, TV, movies, and books.

Self-Check:

Do I make a point of reading the newspaper or preparing topics before new situations where I fear I might feel tongue-tied?

Everyday life can provide fun fodder for discussions with new people. For instance, you could talk about dilemmas you are facing (such as "I can't decide which of two cars to buy..."). Or curiosities (such as "What *is* the theme of this restaurant? They have cacti all over, but the food is Asian"). Or "What was I thinking, I somehow put on two different-colored socks today." Or "Did you ever notice..." Such topics are light and easy, and tap into the everyday experiences that most people can relate to.

Also remember that variety is the spice of first impressions. Oscar Wilde once said: "Conversation should touch everything, but should concentrate itself on nothing." This is especially true for first conversations. You can show more of yourself, and learn more about others, if you make an effort to discuss at least a few different subjects. For example, we once had a First Impressions client who discussed a recent movie, the current tennis tournament, and a novel he was reading. He was stimulating, informative, and entertaining.

Of course, be careful not to jump too quickly from topic to topic. You want to give your conversational partners time to reflect, respond, and relate the topic to their world. But bringing up a few different subjects is likely to make the conversation more stimulating and to open up more opportunities for connection.

The Heavy and the Banal

Some topics are less appealing fare for a first conversation. These fall into the categories of the heavy and the banal.

Heavy Topics

Heavy topics are minefields in first conversations. While relevant to people's lives, they may be too relevant to someone's sense of self. As etiquette dictates, religion and serious political issues are topics that are best eased into slowly or even avoided until you know someone a little better. Ditto on finances. Even though you may not have strong feelings on politics, religion, or money, others may.

These heavies may touch on important personal values and ignite a strong reaction. We all have things that we take seriously and are somewhat rigid about. When someone expresses the opposite view, it's like hearing "You're wrong"—which reflexively makes us feel defensive.

Even if a topic is not presented like a sermon—with the intention of convincing—it may elicit a negative reaction. You might want to be careful about expressing even casual judgment on heavy issues. Take the example of Ashley, a client of ours, who was chatting with an interesting guy at a party. She spoke about her recent trip to Chicago for a friend's wedding. Then she brought up how she finds Catholic weddings so appallingly tedious and boring. Turns out the guy was a religious Catholic, and offended. End of encounter.

It's not that you have to stay superficial. It's just that you will make a much better impression if you start with less charged topics and establish that you respect someone, before you introduce a weightier subject.

Matching Your Intensity As is the general rule in first impressions, it's good form to pay attention to your conversational partners' comfort with topics and in expressing their ideas. We've found that some people are quite open about their beliefs and opinions with strangers. They relish political discussions and talking about ideas. Others need to warm up before they offer any opinion whatsoever. If you can match your "topic intensity," you'll be more comfortable to be around and then, of course, make a better first impression.

Talking Detail: The Banal

On the other side of the spectrum are the banalities. These have too little relevance to others. They won't elicit strong emotions; in fact, they won't elicit any emotions at all. Banalities are the minor details of everyday life, like the traffic jam you just got out of, your company's new policy changes, supermarket sales, the annoying customer service person you dealt with earlier, and the like. Sometimes these details can be on the forefront of your mind and can seem quite fascinating to you. But banalities are boring for most and can be fatal in first impressions. So you might want to make an effort to suppress your desire to "talk detail" with new people, no matter how present in your mind.

For instance, one of our business clients, Mia, told us a story about meeting a woman, Diane, in the lobby of her apartment building as Diane was in the process of moving in. Diane introduced herself and then started telling Mia about the moving company she had used. "They had the nicest woman who answered the phone, and that was what sold me on the company." She then explained that the movers wrapped all her china in newspaper, which surprised her because she thought they would use bubble wrap.

While Diane was friendly, and Mia was glad to meet a new neighbor, Mia felt overwhelmed (and bored) by the minute details of the move.

Self-Check:

Do I often open conversations with whatever is on my mind, even if it's detailed and banal?

SUMMARY

Discussions about the world are an important part of interacting with others during first meetings. How you discuss topics will send strong messages about your social awareness, how you think, and how open-minded you are.

There are infinite topics you can discuss and few set rules as to what is appropriate or inappropriate in a first conversation. However, there are some guidelines that will result in a more positive first impression. If you open up with standard topics, such as the place, the weather, and current events, you will likely be seen as approachable and socially aware. You can then move on to sharing your ideas and opinions in a way that is comfortable and nonthreatening. If you are careful always to give your conversational partner an opportunity to change the topic or follow up, you will likely have a mutually stimulating interaction.

Things go awry in some common ways. One trap that people fall into is talking "at." This includes lecturing, storytelling, sermonizing, and joke telling. You might want to be careful not to force others into a passive or audience mode the first time you meet them. Other traps include talking about heavy subjects or banalities.

How do you introduce and navigate topics? Are you comfortable throwing out a few topics and responding to what others introduce? Do you shy away from any topics in particular? Are you careful to be brief and not fall into telling mode? Think about the percentage of time you talk about subjects of your own initiation versus topics others bring up. If you feel you typically add too little or dominate with your own ideas, try exaggerating in the opposite direction and see how others respond.

As you did in the previous chapters, think about each behavior in the following tables and check off whether you do it usually, sometimes, or rarely.

POSITIVE TOPIC BEHAVIORS

If You Do This:	You May Seem:	Do I Do This?		
		Usually	Sometimes	Rarely
Open with a topic about the immediate surroundings and ease into discussions about ideas	Safe, socially skilled			
Generate a variety of topics	Interesting, stimulating, knowledgeable			
Show interest in topics you know little about	Confident, open, curious			
Check for others' interest in your topics	Flexible, other-oriented, socially aware			
Talk about easy topics, such as current events and observations about everyday life	Nonthreatening, engaging			

COMMON MISCOMMUNICATIONS

If You Do This:	You May Think You Seem:	But You May Seem:	Do I Do This? Usually	Sometimes	Rarely
Listen, but don't add topics to the conversation	Interested, thoughtful	Dull, self-involved			
Focus only on one topic	Passionate	Boring, self-absorbed, lacking in curiosity			
Deliver a lecture on something you know a lot about	Smart, interesting	Bombastic, boring, self-absorbed			
Tell long stories about people or events	Interesting, passionate, sharing	Dull, tedious, boring			
Introduce topics with the goal of convincing others of your way of thinking	Enlightened, smart, passionate	Closed-minded, rigid, controlling			
Dominate the conversation with jokes and humor	Entertaining, lively, funny	Tedious, draining			
Talk about "charged" topics, such as salaries or religion	Passionate, interesting	Insensitive, offensive			
Talk about banalities— details and specifics	Passionate, engaged, informative	Boring, tedious			

SEVEN

Showing Your Cards: Self-Disclosure

In addition to talking about the world around you, most first conversations include sharing personal information—your experiences, feelings, dreams, or challenges—that others wouldn't know if you didn't tell them. While discussing objective topics is your intellectual self-presentation, self-disclosure is your emotional self-presentation.

Self-disclosure is a very powerful thing. Revealing yourself makes you more interesting and likable to others and makes others, in turn, more comfortable opening up to you. Do you remember ever feeling more warmly about someone once they told you a secret about themselves? Understanding the power of self-disclosure can help you control the pace of your relationships. If you want to accelerate a friendship, you can open up and share more. If you want to put the brakes on the relationship, you can hold back.

Even when you want to connect and know that it is a good idea to disclose parts of yourself, you may not know how to do so in a way that will win acceptance. Questions often flash through your mind when you first meet someone: What should I say about myself? Should I hide that? Will they think I'm crazy for revealing this? At times you may hold your cards close to your chest. You might be afraid that if you expose yourself, you'll be seen in a negative light or, worse, be rejected. Other times you may brag, or play all your high cards right away, in the hope of being accepted.

Self-disclosure is the fourth fundamental in first impressions. It is parallel to the third fundamental—the subject matter of first conversations—but is focused on personal rather than impersonal information. In this chapter we outline the process, style, and content of disclosure. Process is the rules of the game, the logistics of disclosing. Style is about how aggressively or passively you play your hand. Do you lay all your cards right on the table, or play them in response to others? And content is the actual cards you play—the specifics of what you share about yourself. Just as with objective topics, we've observed that most people are primarily aware of the content of what they share; they focus on showing their high cards and hiding their low ones. However, how you disclose and your style of sharing say more about you than what you actually share about yourself.

PROCESS: HOW WE DISCLOSE

Conversations evolve in many ways and often meander from the personal to the impersonal and back again. As we described in Chapter 6, we exchange information in ritualistic ways.

The Warm-up

We have a warm-up ritual for how we share personal information. It usually goes like this: We exchange names, talk about how we feel in the immediate situation, where we live, what we do for a living, and our roots. These are the common and basic things we share in most getting-acquainted conversations.

When meeting someone new, you might want to be prepared to field these basic questions about your life. Even if you are not proud of your background or what you do for a living, when you respond in a way that is both honest and positive, others will find you more appealing. You don't have to take yourself too seriously. Having a sense of humor about yourself can help break the ice. For example, if you aren't proud of your telemarketing job, tell people what you like about it. You might say: "You wouldn't believe the conversations I end up having with people!" Or if you're living with your in-laws temporarily, you can say "It's just like *All in the Family*." If you are evasive about this warm-up information, people may suspect you are uncomfortable with yourself or even that you are hiding something. People have active imaginations and may conjure up much worse scenarios than any reality you may be reluctant to share.

Russell, a First Impressions client, came to us because he'd had a series of bad dates and was wondering what to do about it. Russell is an energetic guy with many interesting hobbies; he's a boater and a serious sports competitor. He has a quirky personality and comes across as quite smart and funny. But we discovered that he was also an evader.

In the course of the date, Susan asked Russell what he did for a living. Russell quickly brushed off the question and changed the topic, leaving Susan perplexed. They had a lovely conversation about sailing, but Susan began feeling suspicious that Russell was hiding something. She even found herself wondering whether he was lying about some of his hobbies. During the feedback session, Russell admitted that he gave up his job when he inherited some money. Rather than being up-front about the fact that he wasn't working, Russell undermined his otherwise earnest impression. So, like Russell, if you are evasive with these initial revelations, you may appear awkward or shifty.

Self-Check:

Am I comfortable talking about where I live, my occupation, and my background? Are there basic things about myself that I avoid revealing or significantly distort?

Following the Rules

Most of us are aware of this warm-up ritual and, at least unconsciously, follow it. We share and ask basic information. For good reason; doing so sends the message: "I'm safe and okay." It's a comfortable way to "warm up" to a more meaningful interaction. In essence, it's the conversational foundation on which the rest of a relationship can be built.

Of course, this getting-acquainted ritual is not a set script; every conversation has its own natural flow and order. But if you violate this ritual and start a conversation with whatever is on the top of your mind, or with more obscure personal information, you may come across as interesting or eccentric, but chances are you may also make some people uncomfortable.

Take another of our clients, Betty, a writer from New Jersey. Here's how her date started:

Nick met Betty at a café, smiled, and introduced himself. Nick apologized for being late and asked Betty if she had been waiting long. Betty responded, "No, just ten minutes, and I've been reading the newspaper. There's an article about politics in Mexico. It's particularly interesting to me because I spent some time there after I got out of school. It's a great place, and I still have a lot of memories of it. I got to meet an assistant to the president. . . ."

Betty went on to involve Nick in an intriguing discussion about her experiences in Mexico City. However, Nick felt uneasy with Betty during most of it. He felt catapulted into an intense conversation before she said anything about herself, and he was unsure where the discussion was going. He found Betty to be interesting, but also a bit eccentric and self-absorbed. His discomfort wasn't with what Betty was disclosing; it was with her violation of the getting-acquainted ritual.

Self-Check:

Do I make others comfortable by exchanging common and safe elements—where I am from, what I do—before jumping to topics that are of personal interest to me?

Playing Your Cards

So after the opening ritual, what's next? How do you take the conversation to the next level?

While there are few hard rules about what is appropriate to share of yourself, it's important to understand the power of sharing at least some private information—your background, experiences, feelings, or dreams. Doing so has a big payoff—it makes you more appealing and opens up channels to connection. If you want to get to know someone better, you can share more of yourself and widen the channel.

For instance, Alison, one of our clients, told us about meeting a woman, Lena, at a charity auction. After striking up a conversation, Lena told Alison about how much she liked antiques and that her fantasy was to leave her insurance job and open an antique store. But her husband wouldn't like it, being the practical conservative type. After hearing this Alison felt endeared to Lena and shared that she too would love a change of pace, after working in the same industry for ten years. They swapped fantasy jobs and lifestyles, and told each other about their personal lives. A bond was born between these two, and they went on to become friends.

Be aware that if you hold back and share little of yourself, others won't find easy ways to relate to you, and the channel of connection will be limited. Of course, you may choose to do precisely this if you would like to limit the depth of a relationship with someone. On the other hand, disclosing much more than others do, can make them ill at ease.

SHARING AND LIKING

It's a fact that when you share personal information with someone, it changes how the person feels about you. But how does that work?

Most people understand, at least implicitly, that self-disclosure means something special. It says: I trust you, I value your point of view, and I would like to be closer to you. And it usually fosters reciprocal liking. Indeed, researchers have found that people who disclose more are liked more than people who share less of themselves.

It is also a fact that when you share personal information with someone, it changes how you feel about him. You like him more, just as a result of self-disclosing.

Matching Your Messages: The Disclosure Strip

If you've ever played strip poker, you know how awkward it is when the game isn't progressing at the same rate for both players. Somebody ends up feeling exposed. It's a lot more fun when you both remove your socks before someone takes off his or her shirt. The same is true when revealing personal information. For example, if a man says that he doesn't see his family very often, and you respond with a simple "Oh," he'd likely be left feeling uncomfortable and exposed. On the other hand, it could be equally awkward if your response was "Oh yeah, I haven't seen my mother in ten years, she's a miserable person, and I never forgave her for how she treated me when I was young." That's like you suddenly stripped down to your underwear, putting your new acquaintance ill at ease. Like strip poker, people are most comfortable when both parties evenly match their disclosures.

Self-Check:

Do I pay attention to people's comfort with opening up and then match my level of disclosure to theirs?

SELF-DISCLOSURE STYLE: CUES TO YOUR EMOTIONAL NEEDS

So far we've discussed the process of self-disclosure: the opening ritual and sharing and matching disclosures. However, separate from this process, we all have a style of revealing. Your style is shown by how directly or naturally you bring up information about yourself and in what detail. We've found people tune in to stylistic cues very quickly and weigh them heavily in their evaluation of others. People assume that your self-disclosure style represents your emotional state and needs and that it predicts how you will behave in a friendship or relationship.

Some people are very aware of their self-disclosure style; others are completely unaware of the fact that they even have one. But we all have a style of disclosing. We'll take a look at some of the more appealing and unappealing stylistic approaches.

Let Yourself Be Discovered

Dana, one of our business clients, told us about a new colleague, Victor, she met at the company holiday party. They were standing at the bar waiting to order drinks. Victor commented on the art in the restaurant and asked Dana's opinion of it. He shared his perspective and asked Dana about her taste in art. He followed up with questions about her personal interests. Dana found Victor easy to talk with and asked him more about himself—if he had any special interests or artistic hobbies. Victor explained that he is actually a sculptor and spends his weekends in his studio. Dana was intrigued and asked Victor about his art and how serious he is about it. He explained that while he doesn't make his living at it, he has sold many pieces. He had even had a show recently.

Have you ever discovered an interesting fact about someone by a casual question? It's often much more impressive than having the fact presented to you directly. Victor showed confidence and charm by asking about Dana and then sharing of himself naturally, in response to her interest. Dana also noted that Victor didn't interrupt their conversation about art to talk about his own talents. Dana left the conversation thinking that Victor was someone she'd like to know better.

The Self-Disclosure Agenda

It's normal to highlight our better qualities—such as generosity, financial success, or popularity—when we meet someone for the first time. However, not everyone is as natural as Victor. Sometimes we take the desire to present our fine qualities a little too far and reveal a self-disclosure agenda. That is, we have a list of facts about ourselves that we would like others to know. There are myriad techniques for revealing an agenda. Sometimes we baldly boast, covertly brag, or insert impressive facts parenthetically, and sometimes we move the conversation toward an area where we can display something we'd like to showcase.

Bragging Rites
Inserting positive information about oneself into a conversation is commonly referred to as bragging. Most people realize that blatantly doing so makes them look like they are trying too hard. So they develop techniques to present impressive facts more covertly. For example, there is the common name-dropping technique of sprinkling the conversation with the names of famous or accomplished people we've met. Then there is "credentialing" when we mention our degree or an expensive restaurant we've dined in. Or repeating a compliment

when we share a flattering remark, such as "My client told me I am the most creative person he's ever worked with." These presentations are usually done with the intention of seeming more interesting or important, but often they make one appear to have less of a sense of self.

Self-Check:

Do I have a self-disclosure agenda? Are there specific facts about myself that I try to work into conversations?

A first date or first meeting with a new boss or client is a situation where many people have an agenda. Yet even in more casual social and business interactions, most of us have a little self-disclosure agenda. And yes, your listener may indeed be impressed that you have a Lexus or a management position. But she also might think you are vain and pompous. Or she might sense that you feel insecure about your inherent self-worth and need attention and respect.

By the Way: The Parenthetical Style
Sometimes a self-disclosure agenda is manifested by parenthetical comments that appear related to the conversation but are primarily inserted to tell something about oneself. Alexandra was accomplished at this style.

BRANDON: So what did you do today?
ALEXANDRA: I went shopping for a birthday gift for my sister; I got her a cashmere sweater—*which as far as I'm concerned is the only wool worth wearing.*
BRANDON: Oh, that sounds nice, I am sure she'll like it.
ALEXANDRA: I hope so. And I am making her and my parents dinner this weekend. I'm thinking of making salmon with fresh garlic and snow peas—*I won't eat anything that isn't really fresh and healthy.*

MY FRIEND ONCE MET MADONNA

Connections, even trivial ones, influence our judgment.

People understand the power of associations and use them in first impressions to win favor. One way people do this is by pointing out their associations with successful people, such as mentioning that as a kid they delivered newspapers to a celebrity or went to the same school as a famous politician. They hope to assume some of the characteristics of these famous people or at least shine in the reflected glory of their successes.

Researchers have studied the ways in which people try to capitalize on this reflected glory. They found that people do indeed point out connections with successful people as a way to self-aggrandize. But at the same time, people realize that blatantly flaunting associations can make them appear insincere or unlikable. So they are quite clever about how they mention their connections; they insert them strategically and play them up or down, depending on how they compare themselves to others.

But one thing is clear: If someone name-drops, he is probably trying to impress you.

Here's another example of the parenthetical disclosure technique:

CAROL: So where do you live, Mark?

MARK: I live in Englewood Cliffs, do you know it? It's just outside the city—*I have a great place on two acres*—and it overlooks the river.

CAROL: Sounds beautiful! I'd love a view like that. Are you from there?

MARK: No, I moved out there a few years ago. Before that I lived in the city—*I had a nice place there too, a three-bedroom condo on the twentieth floor. It was fun, but then I missed the outdoors.*

Alexandra and Mark's parenthetical information was interesting. However, this style of disclosure conveys a sense of embellishment and a strong need to impart specific details. The hallmark of parenthetical disclosure is that it is specific (e.g., cashmere) or quantified (two acres, three bedrooms...) when the conversation is more general. So, if you find yourself casually sharing some specific or quantified tidbit about your life, you might be sending an unintended message that you are trying overly hard to impress.

Self-Check:

When revealing information about myself, do I typically wait to be asked before providing impressive details?

As we've outlined, how you introduce information about yourself may seem subtle to you, but it conveys strong messages about your sense of self. You make a much better impression if you let yourself be discovered by others. This means letting go of a self-disclosure agenda and checking your urges to insert specific impressive information about yourself.

CONTENT MATTERS: WHAT TO SHARE

Now that you understand the process of disclosing and the strategic elements, what about content? Exactly what should you share about yourself? There is no specific rule of what to share on a first meeting. Even your alien-abduction story may find an appropriate time and place in a first conversation—if someone introduces the topic, shows real interest, and draws it out of you. But generally speaking, some content conveys specific positive messages while other subjects send more negative ones.

Passions Are Positive

Beth's face lights up when she describes her love of Latin music. Robert's enthusiasm for his job as a police officer is contagious. Louisa loves to talk about her dog Tawny. Personal passions are appealing. Talking about parts of your life about which you feel passionate, whether it's your work, an interest in running, or watching horror films, generally sends very positive messages. That's because when you talk about what excites you, it's like reliving your experience. Your body language—gesturing, smiling, and laughing—is appealing and infectious. By sharing your passions, you also communicate that you are fun to be around and have the ability to take responsibility for your own happiness and well-being. These are very attractive traits.

Blunders Are Sexy

While most of us know about the power of being positive, we don't always realize that showing vulnerabilities also packs a punch. Sharing a weakness or blunder, with a positive sense of humor about it, is a good way to bond with someone. It puts others at ease and makes them feel more comfortable with you. They may even open up with their own challenges and deepen the connection.

Our business client Tommy is a good example. When his consultant asked him about his work, Tommy explained, "I really like the job a lot, and love the people I work with. Which is great for me, since I struggled early in my career and didn't really manage workplace politics too well. I even got fired from my first job!" (Laughing.) The consultant laughed and then shared her own workplace difficulties. "I know what you mean. I once got a really bad review after telling my boss everything I thought he was doing wrong. But I have to say, I've never done that again!"

In sharing this early blunder, Tommy immediately made the consultant feel at ease. By not taking himself too seriously, he projected comfort with himself. Paradoxically, showing a little weakness makes you come across as strong, confident, and very human. This, in turn, makes it more likely that the other person will open up.

Self-Check:

How often do I reveal blunders with people I've just met?

On the other side of the coin, there are some disclosures that send less comforting vibes. These include heavy personal information, as well as everyday complaints and whines.

Oversharing Can be Costly

From time to time we all insert heavy disclosures, especially when an event is fresh in our minds. One client, Harold, a salt-and-pepper-haired businessman in his 40s, "overshared" with his date. In response to Susan's question about his day, he responded, "I just got some test results back!" He then explained that he had prostate cancer but that at the doctor's office that day he learned that the results were better than anyone could have expected, and it looked like he'd beaten it. Susan was supportive and said that he must be incredibly relieved.

Back in the office during the feedback session, Harold's consultant asked him how he felt about sharing this information. Not surprisingly, Harold told her that his test had been foremost on his mind. It was such good news that he wanted to talk about it and thought it was a great way to connect with her. Unfortunately, Harold's news didn't have that effect. While she was genuinely happy for him, Susan felt that the only way she could interact with Harold was to be empathic and supportive. After hearing such news, where could she go from there? Anything Susan might want to talk about, such as her work or the movies she's seen lately, would seem utterly trivial and

RESPECT OR RAPPORT

When it comes to talking about themselves, men and women take different tacks. Men tend to share success stories about their work and finances. Women, on the other hand, talk more about their feelings and personal issues.

A sociolinguist has explained these gender differences as the result of contrasting "interactive goals." Men seek respect, while women seek rapport. She found that these patterns have the same unintended consequences we have observed in our clients. While seeking respect, men may turn women off. And women, seeking likability, may alienate men.

In short, we do not always make the impression we intend on the other sex.

Once we understand the unintended consequences, we can adjust our messages. Men might consider sharing more feelings about people in their life and less about their accomplishments. Women could share more of their successes and less of their feelings. These moves might help us all win the appreciation and respect we desire.

In addition to the content of self-disclosures, men and women differ in how much they reveal about themselves on a first meeting. Most studies show that women open up more than men. However, research also has shown that men recognize that intimate talk creates a deeper relationship and will share more of themselves when they expect or hope to see someone again. They also open up more if they think their female partner likes them or trusts them. So, women: If a man opens up to you on a first meeting, take note. It may indicate that he hopes to continue the relationship or that he thinks you like him.

almost insulting after learning about Harold's news. Although Harold is a very sincere and interesting guy, Susan's main impression of him was of a "man who was recovering from cancer."

Harold's approach may not seem typical. However, once in a while we all share heavy news, not considering the impact it might have on a relative stranger.

Weight Restrictions
What's too heavy? Although there is no specific rule about what personal information is inappropriate to share, as a guideline you may want to think twice about sharing news that forces your conversational partner into a nurturing role. Even important positive information, like Harold's good medical results or the receipt of an award, may oblige your partner to focus on supporting or praising you. Serious negative information is even heavier.

Self-Check:

Do I ever notice a new acquaintance saying things like "Oh, I'm so sorry to hear that" or "How awful"? Do I challenge the conversational "weight restrictions" and give the impression that I want support or empathy?

Remember that since this is a first encounter, what you choose to say will influence your listener's overall impression of you. So, even if the conversation seems to be growing intimate, you may want to resist the urge to launch into a heavy personal topic. You may know you're talking about a temporary issue or a passing problem in your life. But your listener might think you're someone whose life is rife with troubles and burdens, or you are very self-absorbed. Before you disclose, you might want to think about how you want to be thought of: as the person with cancer or as a happy person, a music enthusiast, or a caring dad.

Complaining as Explaining

Complaints are the personal version of the banalities or "detail talk" discussed in Chapter 6 on objective topics. And, like banalities, they are quite unappealing conversational fodder. Even minor negative personal information or complaints can be a turnoff—especially in quantity. For example, one of our clients, Peggy, a banker in her late 20s, talked about feeling tired, never having enough free time, fighting with a friend, and a blow-up with her boss. All this in the space of one hour! Yet interspersed throughout this conversation were really interesting tidbits about her background and her work. During the feedback session, her consultant commented that it seemed like not a lot was going well for her right now. Peggy was surprised to hear this. When he reiterated her fairly extensive list of dissatisfactions, she replied, "Oh, I'm just explaining; those things don't especially bother me, it's just the way they are." Peggy thought she came across as honest and engaged in life. To her consultant, however, Peggy came across as negative, overwhelming, and self-absorbed.

S e l f - C h e c k :

Do I suppress complaints about everyday events when meeting someone new? Or am I all too ready to talk about the mishaps of the day?

We all fall into the complaining-as-explaining trap from time to time, often without knowing it. That's because complaining, like bragging, can be subtle. It's normal and healthy to experience dissatisfactions, and if you seem to have none you may not appear honest or open. But if you complain a lot to someone you just met, you send messages that you are self-absorbed, high maintenance, and even downright boring. Remember, your problems and issues are going to be a lot more interesting to you and your close friends than to a new acquaintance.

Everyone has a lifetime of personal experiences, and they are important parts of who we are. However, you may want to be thoughtful about which ones you share with people you meet for the first time. Your passions and vulnerabilities typically make a positive impression, while heavy personal problems and complaints about your life tend to have the opposite impact.

ANOTHER RECIPE FOR BOREDOM

As we explained, people can be boring in a number of ways.

Researchers have studied boredom by asking participants to listen to conversations between two people and evaluate them. Their findings showed that the most boring topic of conversation is what they call "negative egocentrism," otherwise known as complaining about one's problems.

The study also showed that people make assumptions about boring complainers: that they are much less likable, less friendly, less reliable, and weaker than noncomplainers. People even feel resentment and hostility toward the boring individual. Why such negative reactions to boring people? The authors suggest that it lies in the boring person's violation of a norm that prohibits "the wholesale boredom of others."

In other words, boring other people with your everyday problems is a violation of accepted social norms. We all can minimize our boringness factor by avoiding any urge to complain about our problems to people we've just met.

SUMMARY

As we've just seen, sharing personal information is an important part of a first impression. It helps people get to know who you really are, beyond the basics, and to find common ground. It accelerates a relationship.

Everyone self-discloses in a different way, and there is no one way that feels right for everyone. But as we've outlined, some ways of sharing yourself are more broadly attractive than others. It's appealing to start with the basics and exude comfort and confidence with who you are. When you reveal parts of yourself that you feel passionate and excited about, and avoid heavy information, you appear self-reliant and engaged in life. Remember, this is just the start of a relationship; there will be time to reveal your life story as time goes on. Less is usually more—you can pique your listener's interest so he will want to learn more about you.

What's your self-disclosure style? One way of exploring it is to think of a few positive behaviors discussed in this chapter that seem natural to you. And think of one thing you do that may send less appealing messages. You may think, "Hey, this is who I am and anyone worth knowing will see the real me." However, as this chapter demonstrates, you can display dramatically different "selves" in a first impression—depending on what and how you choose to share.

The following tables list some self-disclosure behaviors and the messages they generally send. Again, think about each behavior in the tables and check off whether you do it usually, sometimes, or rarely.

POSITIVE SELF-DISCLOSURE BEHAVIORS

If You Do This:	You May Seem:	Do I Do This?		
		Usually	Sometimes	Rarely
Share basic information about yourself	Safe, socially appropriate			
Match the depth of your disclosures to what others reveal	Sensitive, understanding, nonthreatening			
Reveal deeper feelings	Sensitive, open to connection, interesting			
Share your passions and interests	Self-reliant, independent, engaged in life			
Share some vulnerabilities and laugh at your mistakes	Self-aware, self-confident, having a sense of humor, down to earth			

COMMON MISCOMMUNICATIONS

If You Do This:	You May Think You Seem:	But You May Seem:	Do I Do This?		
			Usually	Sometimes	Rarely
Share what's on your mind before basic personal information	Interesting and offbeat	Self-centered, eccentric, inappropriate			
Share more than others do	Open, honest, revealing	Burdensome, inappropriate			
Share much less than others	In control, mysterious	Closed, uninteresting, cold			
Volunteer specific impressive information	Important, special	Egotistical, needy of affirmation			
Complain about your problems	Honest, spontaneous	Boring, self-absorbed, critical			

EIGHT

Got Rhythm?: Conversational Dynamics

Now we've covered four of the first impression fundamentals. The first, accessibility, and the second, showing interest, are foundational. The third fundamental, discussing objective topics, and the fourth, self-disclosure, are critical ways to enrich others and connect with them.

In this chapter we take on the fifth fundamental: conversational dynamics. This is all about energy and connection. It's independent of anything you say—it's something that you feel. Imagine for a moment that you are watching two people speak in a language you don't know. Even without understanding their words, you can feel the energy of the interaction, the intensity of the emotion, and how connected the speakers are.

Energy is especially important in a first impression because the content of the conversation tends to be relatively superficial. Most people notice the energy and chemistry of an interaction and appreciate its value yet feel powerless to affect it. You may think that you can't control chemistry. But you can; at least you can control some of it. You can control your own pace and intensity and how you match or complement others' rhythms.

This chapter is about your energy style and conversational dynamics. Your style has two parts. One part is the energy that you put out—how much you talk, how fast, and how loud. The second part of your style is how you synchronize your energy with others—how you take turns, yield or hold the floor, and find a mutually satisfying rhythm.

STYLE PART 1: THE ENERGY YOU PUT FORTH

The first part of your energy style is all about you, independent of your conversational partner. It is how much, how fast, and how loudly you speak. This is energy you bring to an interaction. And it plays a role in how comfortable others feel around you. It can determine whether you put people at ease or create high anxiety.

Floor Space

When you meet someone new, do you hog the floor or hang back? It matters, because the raw quantity of your input plays a role in how enjoyable others find the conversation. Most people want the opportunity to express themselves as well as to listen to input from others. If you satisfy both of these desires, *even when it's not your natural style,* you'll make a better first impression.

Take the example of one of our business clients, Randy, an energetic man in his mid-30s who illustrates the "I'm-really-interested-in-you-now-let-me-talk" style. In the context of a simulated business meeting, Randy spoke with a potential software customer, Carla.

RANDY: Carla, it's so nice to meet you. I've been looking forward to this meeting. I'd love to get to know more about your business needs and then tell you some more about myself and my organization and how we can help you.

CARLA: And I'm happy to meet you, Randy.

RANDY: I've been following your company. Your stock is doing great; you must be doing something right!

CARLA: Yes, business is very good right now.

RANDY: I understand that you may be expanding. We've worked with growing companies like yours. I personally have a lot of experience with companies in the same growth period. Actually, I started out as a sales rep and sold to small to medium-size firms. It was a great experience, and I really learned the industry. I was based in Chicago, which was an exciting city, but now I am glad to be in the South.

CARLA: I see.

RANDY: Let me give you a description of our organization, so you can know something about us. We're headquartered in . . .

The conversation continued in this pattern, so that by the end, Randy had spoken about 80 percent of the time. When his consultant brought this up in the feedback session, Randy explained that while he was aware he was speaking a lot, he thought it was appropriate and had no idea that Carla found it off-putting. He said that he generally concentrates on his key points, not how much he is talking. However, by dominating the conversation, he actually caused his consultant to have the opposite focus. Over time her attention became directed more to how much Randy was talking than to the actual content of his comments, even though his points were important and well articulated. She felt alienated by Randy and had little desire to do business with him.

For most people, a satisfying one-on-one social interaction is one in which the floor is split fairly equally, with each party speaking roughly half of the time. And with a group of three, the satisfying split for most is where each speaks about one third of the time, and so on.

My Way or Yours?

By nature, some people are just talkative; they feel happy when they have the opportunity to speak a lot. Others like to speak less. In a first meeting, then, who determines how the floor is divided—you or your

I LIKE THE WAY YOU MOVE

It's not just what you say or how much you speak. It's also how you move. Your body language plays a role in how likable you appear to strangers

In one study, researchers showed silent videotapes of a person speaking and asked observers to rate the speaker's likability. The researchers then tallied all the different body movements the speaker made and related them to their likability rating. The results showed that certain body movements are more appealing than others, and that men and women were evaluated differently.

They found that for the male speakers, "outward-directed" cues are most likable. That means gestures that are directed away from the speaker and toward the audience or listener. These include outward-directed hand gestures, posture changes, head movements, and smiles. For women, the most likable feature was spontaneous facial expression—that is, how animated the female speaker's face was and how often it changed expression.

So remember, just the way you move your body and face plays a role in how likable you appear to others.

conversational partner? As a rule of thumb, you'll usually make a better impression if you let your partners choose their energy level—by speaking as much or as little as they like—and then follow in a harmonizing way.

You might want to first observe your conversational partner's style and then strive to contribute a *complementary* amount. So, if you're trying to impress a new client or a date who likes to talk a lot, you will probably be more successful if you contribute the complementary amount, even if it's not your natural preference. If he likes to tell lots of stories and speak 90 percent of the time, you will come across more positively if you speak roughly 10 percent and not match him with lots of stories of your own. Likewise, if you are with someone who prefers to speak less than 50 percent, you may want to "pick up the slack" and fill the silences.

If you know your own tendency, you're in a better position to modify it when you want to. One way to monitor yourself is to take a "quantity check" partway through an interaction and think about how much of the time you've been talking relative to others. Then you can strive to make any needed corrections by yielding or asserting yourself to a greater extent in the remainder of the conversation.

Adjusting your style doesn't mean concealing who you are or not "being yourself." Rather, it shows that you are self-aware, sensitive to others, and flexible. Your flexibility is a form of social generosity that will always, at least unconsciously, be registered and appreciated. Remember, making a good first impression is about satisfying others' needs, not your own. As the relationship progresses, you can gradually reveal more of your own style and create a dynamic that is mutually enjoyable.

Self-Check:

Do I know how much I speak compared to others? Do I normally speak proportionately more or less than my share of the time? If so, how strong is my tendency? Is the proportion 90/10, 70/30, and so on? How uncomfortable is it for me to participate at a different level?

Intensity

It's not only *how much* you speak, but the *quality* of the energy you project. That's the difference between how your words sound when you speak them compared to a written text of the same words. Intensity is about how quickly you speak, how long you pause, and your volume of speech.

Shifting Gears

Just as we all have a unique gait, we all have a signature speed in the way we speak. Some people are fast talkers, and some are slow. And we all have a preference for how quickly we'd like others to speak to us.

While we may notice if someone speaks at an uncomfortable pace for us, we may not be fully aware of our own pace and its impact on others. Yet if we speak more slowly than others prefer, we may make them feel impatient or bored. If we speak too fast, we may make them feel uncomfortable, anxious, or even "assaulted."

Take the example of Lily, one of our First Impressions clients, a spirited woman who was a "fast talker." Here's how part of her simulated date went: [We use tight spacing of the letters to indicate fast speech and wide spacing to indicate slow speech.]

LILY: I had this fabulous day yesterday. I went running in the park and then to
     brunch with friends, then a barbecue. Perfect summer day! I love this
     time of year.
NICK (pause): Yeah, me too. Especially afternoon barbecues . . .
LILY: Do you like the beach? I love the sun, even though I know it's bad for
     you. I figure if I sit under a beach umbrella it's okay.
NICK: I do love the beach (pause). My strategy is to go late in
     the day. . . .

In the feedback session, Lily's consultant pointed out that the speed of her speech made him feel quite anxious, even as they were discussing a day at the beach, and he kept trying to slow her down to a pace that was more comfortable for him. Lily said she was aware that she spoke quickly, but didn't realize it was a negative feature. She said she personally finds it annoying when others speak slowly, so she tries to keep a brisk pace. When probed, Lily said she knows how to slow her speech and does when she is with a nonnative speaker, but doesn't think about it otherwise.

What are the signs that you are speaking at an uncomfortable pace for others? One sign is that people may try to exaggerate in the opposite direction (as Nick did) in an effort to change the dynamics of the conversation toward their preferred pace. If you are speaking too fast, your partners may try to slow their speech, create pauses, or even withdraw in discomfort. If you are speaking too slowly, they may finish your sentences, jump in during silences, and speak quickly, all in an attempt to increase the pace of the conversation.

Self-Check:

Am I aware of how quickly I speak relative to others? Do people ever finish my sentences? Do people look like they're having trouble keeping up with me?

When you want to make a good first impression, you might want to be aware how quickly you speak relative to others. If you know yourself to be generally on the fast or slow side, you may want to be especially vigilant for signs of discomfort from others, and adjust accordingly. While it may take a little effort for you to speak faster or slower, doing so will make others more comfortable around you.

Air Space
Pauses, or the space between your sentences, are also part of your energy style. You can speak at a comfortable pace, but if you pause much longer or shorter than others, you can make others uncomfortable. Take these examples from one of our clients. Here's how Bob greeted his consultant:

BOB: Hi,come on in,please have a seat.Excuse me a second I have a couple of things I need to take care of.My boss needs some reports and I have to stop by her office.But I'm really happy to have this time with you.I hope you found my office okay.Can we talk about it over coffee?

JUST MY SPEED

Ever notice that some people make you anxious and others put you to sleep, but some are just right?

It may be a matter of how fast they speak. Researchers have looked at how listeners evaluate speakers who vary in speech rate. Turns out that there was no rate of speech that was universally appealing to listeners. Rather, listeners had a preference for speakers whose *rate of speech was most like their own*. Fast speakers liked other fast speakers, and slow talkers liked other slow talkers. Further, participants assumed that people who spoke at the same rate as they did had positive personality traits; they assumed they were kind, likable, pleasant, intelligent, and confident.

Our impressions of others are influenced by how similar they are to us, even in qualities such as rate of speech. So, from a first impression standpoint, you'll likely be perceived more positively if you adjust your speed of speech to match your conversational partner's.

Bob barely paused at all; he didn't give his consultant a chance to "get a word in edgewise." This style can come across as controlling, and even selfish, because it shuts out others and denies them the opportunity to express themselves. It also creates an atmosphere of anxiety and frustration.

Imagine that Bob spoke the same words but left really long pauses between his sentences:

BOB: Hi.... Come on in......... Please have a seat...............
Excuse me a second..... I have a couple of things I need to take care of............ My boss needs some reports and I have to stop by her office...................... But I'm really happy to have

this time with you...I hope you found my office okay............Can we talk about it over coffee?

In this hypothetical example, the long pauses created a "low-voltage" atmosphere. If you pause too long, you may create an awkward conversational rhythm.

Self-Check:

How long do I pause between my words and sentences? Do I give others space to jump in? Do I pause so long that others have a hard time staying focused?

If you pause for too short *or* too long a time, you may disengage your conversational partners. While managing your pauses sounds straightforward, sometimes our clients are not sure how to adapt their speed. To slow down, we advise that they just apply conscious effort to pause longer, and allow their conversational partner more space to jump in. Speeding up can seem harder, but it's really listening with your whole mind to what the other person says and building on it. It can mean letting go of a desire to choose your words carefully and instead prioritizing the flow of your speech.

Can You Hear Me?

Another important energy quality is volume—how loudly or softly you speak. Most people speak in a volume that is matched to others and vary their volume naturally in accordance with the background noise.

However, you may have a general tendency to speak at a volume that is different from the norm. If you speak too loudly, you may think you come across as natural, confident, and fun. But you may instead communicate arrogance, a need for attention—as if you want to impress not only your companion, but also the people at the next table and across the room—or a simple lack of social awareness. You risk being categorized as a loud person, which is often associated with a cluster of negative traits, such as being self-centered, brash, and annoying. If you speak too softly, you may think you are being demure and sensitive, but you may come across as lacking in confidence, shy, or unenthusiastic. And speaking softly sometimes can come across as "controlling" if you force the listener to work to hear you—by moving closer and asking you to repeat yourself.

How do you know if you need to modulate your volume? Even if it feels as if you're talking normally, if you are speaking at a volume that differs from your listener's preference, you may come across as a loud or quiet person. Sometimes people give indirect feedback when they are "volume uncomfortable" by exaggerating in the other direction in an effort to try to bring the volume to their comfort level. So, if you often find others responding to you in a low voice they may be giving you indirect feedback that you are speaking too loudly, and vice versa. Of course, you don't want to make others resort to "shushes" or asking you to please speak up.

Self-Check:

Am I naturally loud or quiet of voice? Do I adjust my volume to match others with a different volume?

STYLE PART 2: SYNCHRONIZING WITH OTHERS

Now we've explored the elements of your personal energy style—how much you speak and your intensity. Sometimes it's hard to know these things about yourself. If you have any doubts, ask a friend how you come across in these ways.

The next step is synchronizing your energy style to that of someone else. Making a good first impression is very much about how you attend to and synchronize your rhythm to others. This is where the chemistry comes in. It's like playing music with others—you listen, respond to their pace and melody, and create a dynamic.

Back and Forth

One really simple and key way that you synchronize with others is by good old-fashioned turn-taking. Though this sounds simple, even some highly socially skilled people sometimes fall out of step with people they don't know.

Let's look at the basics. Turn-taking is more than contributing an equal amount to the conversation. For example, in a ten-minute conversation, you could speak for the first five minutes, and then your conversational partner could speak the second five minutes. That conversation would look like this, with the x's representing you speaking and the y's representing your conversational partner:

xxxxxxxxxxxxxxxxxx, yyyyyyyyyyyyyyyyyy

While this is an extreme example, sometimes conversations never find the right flow, like Randy and Carla's conversation in the example earlier. That looked more like this:

xxxx, y, xxxxx, y, xxxx, y, xxxxxx, y

In this situation, you, like Randy, may feel that the interaction is balanced, because you're "taking turns." However, you may unknowingly be throwing off the balance by speaking *too long* during your turn. It can suck the energy out of the interaction.

As a rule of thumb, if you speak more than three or four sentences in a row, you risk losing the connective energy with someone. In first encounters in particular, short is sweet. In the *x* and *y* vocabulary, short and sweet would look like this:

$$xx, yy, x, y, x, y, xx, yy, x, y, x, y, xx, yy$$

For most people, an engaging interaction is one with balanced turn-taking, where both parties are evenly matched in how long they speak. However, even if your conversational partner tends to speak in long stretches, you are more likely to make a positive impression if you complement him by being brief, rather than matching his length.

HARMONIZING BODIES

You synchronize with your conversational partner in two key ways. One is with your verbal repartee. And the other is with your physical movements.

But how do you physically harmonize? What are the steps? Psychologists looked at many elements of nonverbal coordination and found three that are key. One is coordinated smiling. If you smile together, you are usually in harmony. The next is gesturing, as in using your hands to make a point while you are speaking. Finally, gaze matters. If you gaze at each other at the same time and look attentive while listening, it fosters good rapport. It's about responding and respecting. You smile back, you watch and listen, you take your turn. Together you find a rhythm.

Harmonizing also fosters liking. Researchers have found that when you mimic the movements of your conversational partner—even when you do so unconsciously—it makes the interaction smoother and makes you like each other more. The authors propose that this "chameleon" behavior helps create and maintain relationships and "serves the basic human need to belong."

Self-Check:

How long do I speak when it's my turn? Is my input shorter or longer than others'? Can I adapt, and speak for longer or shorter times?

After You: How to Respond to Interruptions

Interruptions are a part of life. Despite all your attention to appropriate turn-taking, it's inevitable that, at times, you will speak at the same time as someone else or someone will interrupt you. And, commonly, there is a pause during which you must decide whether to assert yourself or let the other speak. While you may have a really, really important point to make, you will most likely make a much better first impression if you yield. This doesn't mean you should never assert yourself, but rather that, by yielding, you will appear more interested in what your conversational partner has to say than in your own thoughts.

While there are some gender differences, with men seeing interrupters more positively than women do (see the following research box), it's safe and polite to avoid talking over others the very first time you meet them. People are more drawn to those who hang on their every word than to those who speak over them. Yielding is charming. Even when you have the floor, you can yield to their impatience. If someone appears restless—for example, by saying "uh-huh, uh-huh, uh-huh"—it's a good signal to wrap it up and see what she has to say.

SUMMARY

Apart from anything you say, your energy and ability to synchronize with others will influence how you are perceived. People make assumptions about you by the energy you put forth in a first meeting.

INTERRUPTERS: FRIEND OR FOE?

There are rules about turn-taking in conversations. He talks, you listen, you talk, he listens, and so on. But sometimes people talk over and interrupt others. How is that usually perceived? Does the interrupter appear interested and excited, or is he seen as controlling?

To explore this question, researchers recorded conversations between two speakers, one of whom interrupted the other. Participants listened to the tapes and rated the speakers on personality characteristics.

Reactions to the interrupter turned out to depend on the gender of the listener—and *not* on the gender of the interrupter. Female listeners saw the interrupters negatively—as pushy, disrespectful, and unpleasant. Male listeners, however, had a more positive view of interrupters than women did. They were more likely to see interrupters as expressing liking, interest, and agreement.

The authors suggest, "Men may sometimes be trying to show interest, engagement, and understanding by interrupting, but women may often misconstrue this as a sign of disrespect and desire to overpower. By understanding the different rules used by men and women, such misinterpretations might be minimized."

You may be categorized as engaging or difficult to connect with based on how much and how intensely you speak.

Consciously or unconsciously, people note how much you speak relative to them, your pace, and how loudly you talk. Most important, they notice how comfortable you are to interact with from their energy vantage point, that is, how easily you align with their style. They notice whether you take turns and create a dynamic that is comfortable for them. Even though you may implicitly understand the norms, nerves or the discomfort of a first meeting may affect how much and how intensely you speak.

Importantly, deviating from the norms of conversational dynamics and not aligning with others incurs a social cost to them and can cause them an uncomfortable and unpleasant experience. On the other hand, if you align with their dynamic, others may get a connecting feeling from you. They may not recognize it specifically as your "energy" skills; they'll just get a warm impression of you.

If you can let go of your own preference and go with the flow of your conversational partners, you will likely make a better impression than if you try to bring others to your energy style. Being flexible in this way demonstrates that you are perceptive, other-oriented, and socially generous. And you will make people feel more comfortable and satisfied in your company.

Read through the following tables and think about each behavior. Check off whether you do it usually, sometimes, or rarely. As we mentioned, your energy style is an area where it can be hard to see yourself the way others do. A good way to gain self-knowledge is to ask a trusted friend whether you sometimes talk more than your share and if you speak faster or slower, louder or softer than others.

POSITIVE CONVERSATIONAL DYNAMICS BEHAVIORS

If You Do This:	You May Seem:	Do I Do This?		
		Usually	Sometimes	Rarely
Allow others the opportunity to express themselves and to get input from you	Engaged, interested, and interesting			
Pay attention to how much others like to speak, and add a complementary amount	Perceptive, socially generous, easy to communicate with			
Keep your input short	Other-oriented			
Speak at the same pace as your conversational partner	Likable, easy to converse with			
Speak at the volume that your conversational partner prefers	Comfortable, confident			
Follow regular turn-taking	Engaging, sensitive			
Yield to interruptions	Interested in others, socially generous			

COMMON MISCOMMUNICATIONS

If You Do This:	You May Think You Seem:	But You May Seem:	Do I Do This?		
			Usually	Sometimes	Rarely
Speak more quickly or pause more briefly than others	Interesting, energized	Emotionally draining, alienating			
Speak more slowly or pause longer than others prefer	Relaxed, comfortable, thoughtful	Boring, tedious			
Speak more loudly than others	Self-confident, fun, interesting	Bombastic, self-satisfied, offensive			
Speak more softly than others	Demure, socially aware	Shy, lacking in self-confidence, controlling			
Speak much more than others	Interesting, informative	Self-absorbed, difficult to connect with			
Talk longer than others during your turn	Sharing appropriately, interested	Draining, not connecting			
Interrupt others or fail to yield	Interesting, energetic	Uninterested, self-absorbed, controlling			

NINE

How You See the World: Perspective

Now we move on to the sixth first impression fundamental. This fundamental is about your perspective: how you see yourself and the world you live in. What kind of perspective on life do you project? Do others see you as relaxed or alarmist, as in control or as a victim? Do you see yourself as better than or lesser than others?

Perspective can be obvious or subtle. It can be conveyed without words or with a single adjective. But people pick up on your perspective quite readily, even in a first conversation, and then, based on it, make assumptions about your overall personality.

Your perspective on life is an integral part of you. Of course, you may not want to change how you feel about yourself or see the world. But there are a couple of important reasons you might want to examine the perspective you convey when you meet someone for the very first time. First, people will make strong judgments about your personality based on it. So you'll want to be sure that the perspective you project is in line with your real perspectives on life. Second, if you know what elements of perspective are perceived positively, you can tweak the way you present yourself when you want to make a good impression.

Your perspective is part of what you share about yourself, something that is usually indirectly conveyed. People rarely state their perspective in a straightforward manner, as in "I'm an optimist, inflexible about some things, and feel myself to be just a bit superior to most other people." Rather, it's communicated subtly in how you demonstrate how you feel about yourself, how you see yourself in life, and how you feel about yourself relative to others.

In this chapter we outline how you present your perspective style and content. Your style is the way you project your sense of self. It's about how flexible or rigid you come across and how much you minimize or "catastrophize" events. It's also about whether you project a sense of superiority or inferiority and whether you see yourself as in control or as a victim. The content of your perspective is the actual things you talk about—whether they are positive or negative, uplifting or serious.

STYLE: SHOWING YOUR SENSE OF SELF

Going with the Flow

One part of your perspective style is your flexibility. How flexible you appear conveys something about you and how you see the world. Part of this is how you express your opinions and ideas, as discussed in Chapter 6. But it's more than that. It's about how you respond to the world in the moment and how you react to unexpected events.

Life is full of flux. You can react to it by going with the flow or resisting it. Most people like some control and make plans to minimize the uncertainties in life; for example, they leave a little extra travel time, order tickets in advance, make dinner reservations, and keep their car in good working order. But outside of our control, stuff happens. You may be relaxed about most things but have a "hot button"—something that you are more rigid about than other things. Perhaps you particularly hate to be delayed, or you may be sensitive to heat and not able to tolerate it when the air conditioning isn't working.

People judge you by how you react to situations out of your control, and strangers judge you most harshly. Strangers lack the experience of seeing you in the whole range of situations and will make judgments about you based only on how you react to the single situation they observe.

The following are some "flexibility" experiences our clients and friends have recounted:

John and Paul are on a first date. John picks a restaurant in his neighborhood. Paul comments on the nice decor and compliments John on his stylish shirt. Things are going well. John orders the chicken piccata, Paul the steak au poivre. The waiter apologizes and says that they are out of the chicken piccata, and John gets ruffled. He complains that that is the only dish he really likes on the menu, the reason he goes there. Isn't there anything they can do? Don't they have any chicken at all left? He argues with the waiter for a few minutes and finally states he'll only have an appetizer and some bread. Paul is uncomfortable and tries to put the experience aside in his mind, but he finds it hard to connect with John after witnessing that inflexible moment.

Let's imagine the situation unfolded differently following the announced lack of piccata:

JOHN: No chicken piccata! That's my favorite! Really? Oh, well. I guess this is my night to try something new. Do you have any specials?

This approach shows passion yet flexibility.

Here's another experience, taking place at a party between two unacquainted guests:

CHRIS: You said you were a friend of Paula's?
JEREMY: No, I'm a friend of Robin's.
CHRIS: I heard you say Paula.
JEREMY: I'm sorry, perhaps you misheard, it's loud in here. I don't know Paula.

CHRIS: Well, you said it.
JEREMY: Okay, whatever.

Chris was displaying a rather rigid approach to a minor comment, out of proportion to the situation. Here's a less rigid unfolding:

CHRIS: You said you were a friend of Paula's?
JEREMY: No, I'm a friend of Robin's.
CHRIS: Oh, I must have been mistaken, I know Robin as well....

Arguing with a stranger will get you nowhere. It's more appealing to admit to or assume you made a mistake, even when you feel certain that you are right.

A colleague of ours was at the airport, waiting in line to check in at the gate. The man in front of her chatted her up. He asked if she had heard the breaking news on the airport TVs. They were engaged in a fun discussion of current events when it was the man's turn to check in.

MAN: I believe I have an aisle seat.
GATE AGENT: I'm sorry, sir; we don't have any more aisle seats left.
MAN: But my travel agent told me that she reserved one for me.
GATE AGENT (looking at monitor): I have no record of that. I wish I
    had an aisle for you, but I don't. All I have left are middle seats, or
    I can get you a window in aisle 23.
MAN: I can't believe this! You people are so incompetent! This takes
    the cake! Can't you keep anything straight? Just give me whatever.
GATE AGENT: Sir, I'm very sorry. There is nothing I can do.

The man grabbed his boarding pass with a scowl, then turned to his new acquaintance to ask if she would like to join him for a drink before the flight. Put off by the man's reaction to his seating news, she declined his offer, pretending she had calls to make.

Like John and the chicken piccata, this man catastrophized a situation and alienated a new acquaintance. Here's a more flexible version:

GATE AGENT: All I have left are middle seats, or I can get you a window in aisle 23.

MAN: Are you sure you couldn't find anything? I hate the idea of sitting in a middle or window seat. Nothing you can do? I'll have to take it up with my travel agent. Well, a window would be better than a middle seat.

While these examples may seem a little extreme, you've probably had an "inflexible moment" or two in your life. Maybe it's a personal hot button, or maybe it was after you had a really difficult day and something ended up not going your way. Being combative serves only one purpose—letting off steam. But it makes everyone else uncomfortable.

In general, presenting a flexible style suggests you are "low social maintenance," while rigidity suggests that you see yourself as superior and entitled. When you are rigid, it's like saying that your needs are more important than others', or that you are childish and lacking in self-control. As always, we aren't advocating that you change your personal preference, but just be aware of the social costs of expressing it. If you want to make a positive impression on someone you've just met, you may want to make an effort to be just a notch more flexible than you usually are.

Self-Check:

What are my flexibility hot buttons? What trips me up? Is it about space, food, time, personal comfort? How do I react when a button is pressed?

Status: One-Up, One-Down, or Equal

Another element of your perspective style is how you present your sense of status. Do you come across as arrogant or inferior? Do you make people feel similar or equal to you? Do you present a different perspective when you are with close friends than new acquaintances?

The pressure of a first meeting can have a big impact on the way you present yourself. For one thing, you may think that you have to compensate for something you feel deficient in or insecure about, such as your talent, appearance, smarts, money, or professional success.

Self-Check:

What personal dimension am I most insecure about? Do I often compare myself to others in this area? Does it change the way I present myself?

There are three ways you can present yourself relative to others: from the one-up position, the one-down position, or a position of parity. In general, people feel comfortable with someone that they feel similar and equal to. Yet some people are a little insecure in first meetings, and equal is not enough. They may feel uncomfortable being in an inferior position of any kind, and will be more open to you if they feel that they are at least a notch superior to you. So if you want to make a good impression, the safest approach is to humble yourself just a bit and find similarities with others.

Status Style 1: The One-Up Position
If you don't know how to present your status in a first meeting, your first instinct may be to "look down" and present yourself as having a superior position relative to others. You may try this approach when you want to make a good impression. While it may be appropriate if you are invited to a meeting for your expertise, it's ineffective in most other situations. It can make others feel inferior, or it may make you appear arrogant or needy of affirmation. It actually lessens the chance of making a positive connection.

You can convey superiority in a number of ways. One way is bragging, as we described in Chapter 7. Another is with posturing, by saying, in essence, "I'm better than you." You may overtly or subtly elevate yourself by disparaging other people or by conveying that you are smarter, more successful, more socially connected, or more important than your conversational partner. Here are some ways we've observed people express their superiority.

Proactive Positioning: Establishing Your Platform Some people like to open up a dialogue by establishing their rank. It can mean establishing your professional position, as in "I head up the East Coast division" rather than "I work out of the Boston office." Or your financial position: "We live on the water" rather than "We live in Park Grove."

Reactive Positioning: I'll Top That! This is looking for and reacting to rank by matching or topping it. As in when someone says: "My husband and I went on a cruise last month," and you say "Oh, we've been on a few cruises, but now we like to do more interesting things; we just went on a safari." A less reactive approach response could be "I love cruises too, where did you go?"

Self-Check:

Do I ever try to communicate my social or financial status to strangers? Do I try to establish it right off the bat, or respond to others' expression of rank?

Sometimes, just by being yourself, you may intimidate others. Or you may have an understated superiority and unknowingly make others ill at ease in your presence. In any event, it's good to know the signs that you are making others uncomfortable. One common sign that you are coming off as superior is that others start "reactionary posturing," or trying to one-up you. Or they may change the topic to something where they feel less inferior. Or they may start self-monitoring, physically stiffen, and withdraw from the conversation.

YOUR BODY AND YOUR STATUS

People communicate their status to others through their body language. If someone feels himself to be in a superior position to others, he will probably display different body language than if he feels inferior.

Psychologists studied this phenomenon by assigning unacquainted participants to be "teacher" or "student" and then observed their behavior. Those in the higher-status role of teacher took up more space with their bodies, talked more, tried to interrupt more, and touched and pointed more than did their lower-status conversational partner. When the roles were reversed, and the teacher became the student to the same person, their body-language patterns changed to reflect their new status.

So, you may be showing others how you feel about yourself, and how you feel about them, just by the way you move and use space.

Status Style 2: The One-Down Position

If you don't want to appear superior, you can present yourself in a one-down position. There are a couple of ways of doing so. One is from a position of shame or inferiority. As most people know, this is not the most charming perspective to convey. In our experience, people seldom put themselves down directly during a first meeting. They don't say, "I'm really not that important or interesting." But they might compare themselves to you or someone else, as in a snide comment such as "This woman is *really* important, she's a corporate lawyer," as an expression of discomfort. More often people communicate an inferior perspective by shying away from someone they feel intimidated by.

You may not always know how to respond gracefully when you are feeling intimidated. Instead of reactively posturing or withdrawing, you can show confidence by acknowledging expressed status. If someone says she is a corporate lawyer and you feel inferior to her, you can always address her directly about it and say "That's great, that must be an interesting job. How do you like it?"

Modesty Methods A more appealing way to look up to others is from a position of modesty or a slight lowering of your status. Modesty can go a long way. One reason is that some people are uncomfortable being in any one-down position at all, so if you humble yourself, you make them more comfortable around you. Another reason is that humility and modesty are appealing qualities in and of themselves. When you are modest, you convey that you don't take yourself too seriously and are not self-absorbed. It makes you accessible and easy to connect to.

Just as you may want to stretch your mood up one notch when you meet someone, you may want to lower your status level down just a notch to make a positive impression. There are a number of ways you can act humble. A good start is by introducing yourself in a straightforward or unembellished way, as in "I work in the apparel industry" rather than "I own a chain of clothing stores." You can also use lighthearted humor or self-deprecation, as in "I'm the worst at finding my way around, I hope I don't embarrass you...." You can also admit to mistakes or blunders, as we mentioned in Chapter 7, as a way of showing some vulnerability or human weakness. For example, "What a fool I am! I can't believe I forgot to bring...." Admitting to your errors or shortcomings shows character strength and that you take responsibility for yourself rather than blaming others—as long as you do not consistently undermine yourself.

Another way of humbling yourself is to shift the focus off of you. You can ask others' opinions about things or reinforce others' positive features. You can find a way to elevate someone relative to you by pointing out what you admire or like about her or that you find her opinions interesting. If you know you are impressive in some way, you can compliment others in the same dimension. For example, if you are stylish and attractive, you can tell others when you like their outfit or style.

Self-Check:

Do I make a conscious effort to be just a little modest about my positive features when I meet someone new?

Status Style 3: The Parity Position
Humility is safe, and a good start. But parity is another positive approach. If you present yourself as if you said "I'm just like you," it's like looking eye-to-eye with your partner. Establishing a comfortable rapport and finding equal ground is the essence of a positive connection and what people generally strive for.

What's the best way to get there? With people who don't know one another, it can take some "feeling out" before you find yourself on equal footing. Even if you present yourself as on par with someone, he may feel superior or inferior to you. If you think someone finds you superior, you may want to demonstrate your modesty. You can make him comfortable by presenting yourself in an understated way, using humorous self-deprecation, and shifting the focus from yourself. If you feel that someone sees you in an inferior position— if, for example, you are lower on the totem pole at work—you may establish parity not by posturing or one-upping, but by finding something you have in common, whether it is parenting, gardening, or sports, and pointing out where you share attitudes or a point of view.

THE INVISIBLE INFLUENCE

Do you think you make completely conscious decisions about how you present yourself, what you say, and what you focus on? You don't. There is a strong unconscious influence on your behavior: how other people present themselves.

To demonstrate this, researchers interviewed college students about their experiences and feelings about school. But before the interview, the participants were shown a description of another person's experience that was either quite positive ("I've had some wonderful friendships and roommates...") or negative ("I've had some soured relationships...").

The participants were strongly influenced by the description they read before their interview. Those who read about the wonderful friendships appeared much more positive about their own experiences and feelings than those who read about the soured relationships. *But they were completely unaware of the influence.* When asked how they thought they came across, all participants felt they came across neutrally; they didn't think they presented a biased impression of their feelings in any way.

Like these research participants, you probably are unaware of how others affect the way you present yourself. And you may not be aware of how strongly you influence others in the same way. You have the power to bring out the positive or the negative in someone, without the person even knowing it.

Control Issues

So far we've outlined some elements of perspective style—flexibility and status. Another aspect of style has to do with "control"—that is, how much or little control you appear to have over your life or others. "Taking" control versus "having" control conveys very different things.

The Overcontrolling Approach

Take the example of our business client, Doug, a 55-year-old manager in the pharmaceutical industry. Doug had a tendency to take over a situation and control the direction and the details. Here's how his lunch meeting opened:

DOUG: Hi, so nice to meet you. Tell me about yourself. Where are you from?

CONSULTANT: I'm from Pennsylvania originally, and you?

DOUG: I'm from California myself. So, excuse me, but let's order our food first so we can get our order in as quickly as possible. I've been here before; I recommend the sandwiches, most of the other dishes aren't that good. I suggest the roast beef or the chicken avocado.

CONSULTANT: Hmm. Well, I haven't really had a chance to look.

DOUG: You can take a look, but as I said, the best things are the roast beef and the chicken.

CONSULTANT: I'll just take a quick look at the menu.

DOUG: It's a bit busy here; I'm going to ask if we can move to that table over there.

CONSULTANT: I'm fine here, really.

Doug's style was bossy. He not only managed the dynamics of the conversation, but also tried to influence what his consultant ate and what table they were sitting at. When the consultant brought this up later, Doug explained that he was just trying to be helpful. He wanted her to have a tasty lunch and wanted the setting to be as nice as possible. He said he likes to be able to take care of things and make others happy. However, what Doug didn't realize was that his "helpfulness" actually made his consultant feel restrained and not able to express herself comfortably.

The Out-of-Control Approach

The other side of this spectrum is presenting yourself as not in charge of situations—or your life. Take our client Vivian. Unlike Doug,

Vivian presented herself as having little control over her life's direction and details.

NICK: Where do you live, Vivian?
VIVIAN: I'm living in Forest Hills. I love the neighborhood. I have a condo there, which is nice but too small. I've been planning on moving into something larger, but I'm waiting for my ex to pay me what he owes me. So I'm stuck.
NICK: Oh, that's too bad.
VIVIAN: Yeah, I know. He really took me for a ride.
NICK: Sorry to hear. So, do you work in the city?
VIVIAN: No, I work in Long Island. I was supposed to be transferred to the city. But my boss is dragging his feet. He promised me the transfer last year.
NICK: Well, business is slow where I'm working too.
VIVIAN: I wish that were the case, we are so busy! My boss is keeping me in the Long Island office because he knows I get things done.

In the feedback session, Vivian's consultant pointed out that it seemed that there were a lot of things working against her, like her ex and her boss. While there may be legitimate challenges in her life, her consultant showed Vivian that she came across as victimized by others—as someone who may not take responsibility for herself and may not have the emotional energy to fulfill others' needs.

While you may not feel as victimized as Vivian does, you may carry some resentments that you reveal on a first meeting. It could be a complaint about the contractor who never finished your home improvements, the airline that lost your luggage, your friend who ditched you, whatever. While these may be legitimate, and emotionally important to you, when you focus on such experiences in a first meeting, you send the message that you may be someone who looks to blame others, rather than accept personal responsibility for your life events.

The In-Control Approach

Presenting a perspective of being in control communicates that you can take care of yourself, can take charge of your life, and have energy to attend to others' needs. It's different from Doug's controlling style in that it suggests an independence without a drive to change or influence others.

For example, Vivian would have come across as in control rather than a victim if she hadn't pointed fingers. She might have said that she liked her apartment, yet was hoping to move to a larger place. Vivian may truly feel that she has been victimized by some people in her life. But she would make a better first impression if she focused on what she is doing for herself.

CONTENT: WHAT YOU CHOOSE TO FOCUS ON

We've outlined how you communicate your perspective. Now we'll talk about the content of conversation that communicates perspective—how positively or negatively you focus, and the danger of overdoing it.

In Chapters 6 and 7 we discussed conversational content that is objective or personal. Here we focus on content that reveals your perspective.

Is It Cloudy or Bright? The Outlook You Convey

In every situation there is beauty and humor, as well as ugliness and banality. You have a choice of what to focus on and discuss with others. Your overall focus may label you as a carefree optimist or a selfish curmudgeon.

Here's an experience of our friend Mary Jane, who was visiting some friends at their lake house on a beautiful summer day. She and her hosts were hanging out on the deck, reading magazines and sipping iced tea when a neighbor, Amelia, wandered over to say hello. Amelia was graceful and warm, and joined them on the deck. She engaged them in conversation, commented on the lovely day, and asked them what they thought about a local event. Mary Jane found her to be an enjoyable person whom she'd be happy to spend the afternoon chatting with. Another neighbor, Perry, wandered over. Perry introduced himself and joined the conversation. Soon he launched into a complaint about the motor boats and how loud and rude they were, and the environmental effects of the pollution. Mary Jane found herself stuck listening to this man's diatribe against boaters. While he had sound arguments, she found him to be a bitter, unpleasant person. He was inflicting a social cost on her, by robbing her of the opportunity to enjoy the beautiful afternoon and her other companions' conversation.

What you choose to talk about in any situation can send strong messages about you. When you focus on the negative, like Perry, you suggest that you are a glass-half-empty type of person and likely to be a social burden. If you focus on the positive or the funny, especially in a mundane or unpleasant situation, you communicate that you can take things lightly and will be a social asset.

Pollyanna Perils
Most people like a positive spin. They will find you more endearing if you speak more of the good in a situation than the bad. But that said, being a pure Pollyanna—speaking exclusively of wonderful things and piling on positive adjectives—may raise alarm in some people's minds.

Here's an experience a friend of ours, Leon, had at a party.

COURTNEY: Isn't the food fabulous! Did you taste this cheese?
LEON: Yeah, it's delicious.
COURTNEY: Oh, I love it. The food is great, and the people here are so nice. Hi, I'm Courtney.
LEON: I'm Leon. So, are you a friend of Judy's?
COURTNEY: Yes!! Isn't she great? I adore her parties. Have you been to any before?
LEON: No, we just met; I just started working with her.

YOU'RE GLUE

People are naturally interesting conversational fodder. We like to talk about ourselves and other people we know. In a first conversation, we may describe ourselves, our children, and our coworkers, and talk about politicians and celebrities. But beware what you say about others. Turns out, you're glue. What you say about others bounces back and sticks to you. Psychologists call this "trait transfer."

For example, in a casual conversation you may joke about your couch-potato brother and his snack food habit. But your new acquaintance may leave the conversation thinking that *you* are lazy.

Turns out, we're all prey to such mental muddles. We spontaneously and mindlessly confuse what people tell us about themselves and what they tell us about others. Luckily, it's also true of positive traits. If you describe your brother as someone who loves to write poetry, *you* may be remembered as a creative person.

COURTNEY: She must be a joy to work with. I work with some wonderful people too. They're all so nice.

LEON: ... That's great.... Uh, I need to get another drink. Catch you later, Courtney.

Leon definitely found Courtney upbeat, but also rather shallow and tedious. Because of her exclusively positive commentary, he didn't find her interesting to talk with. If you, like Courtney, talk about everything as being absolutely wonderful, people may question your sincerity or even your intellectual depth.

So how can you be positive but not look shallow? It's a matter of order and balance. As we mentioned earlier, starting with a positive makes a good impression. But then you can balance your positive comments with your positive, neutral, or critical perspectives as they emerge naturally. Or ask others their opinions. Courtney could have stopped her ongoing trumpeting of positive commentary to talk about something she wasn't fabulously excited about or to ask Leon his perspective on things, how he felt about his new job with Judy, and so on.

SUMMARY

Others readily pick up on your perspective on life. It's evident by your degree of flexibility, how much or how little control you appear to command over your life, and how you position yourself relative to others. While it may seem subtle to you, people will judge you on it and use it to make assumptions about your personality.

There are some common ways in which you may miscommunicate your perspective. You may react strongly to the situation or to something that annoys you. Or the discomfort of a first meeting or the feeling of being compared to others may make you alter the way you present yourself relative to others. Or you inadvertently focus on a passing negative event, suggesting to new people that you are a negative person in general.

If you want to be appealing to others, you could try to stretch your flexibility presentation just a bit, humble yourself just a bit, and focus on the positives.

What kind of perspective do you convey? Flexible or rigid? Superior, inferior, or on par with others? Positive or negative? Think about your style as you read through the following behaviors. Check off whether you do them usually, sometimes, or rarely.

POSITIVE PERSPECTIVE BEHAVIORS

If You Do This:	You May Seem:	Do I Do This?		
		Usually	Sometimes	Rarely
Are flexible when faced with undesired circumstances	Easygoing, other-focused, low maintenance			
Are modest about your position relative to others	Comfortable to be around, accessible, connecting, down to earth			
Show responsibility for your own life situation	Independent, confident, in control			
Focus on the positive and lighthearted	Pleasant, optimistic, entertaining			

COMMON MISCOMMUNICATIONS

If You Do This:	You May Think You Seem:	But You May Seem:	Do I Do This?		
			Usually	Sometimes	Rarely
Act inflexibly to unexpected events	Determined, appropriately demanding	Needy, entitled, high maintenance			
Present yourself as superior to others	Important, impressive	Intimidating, insecure			
Present yourself as very inferior to others	Modest, endearing	Awkward, lacking confidence			
Control the situation and others' actions	Generous, helpful, in command	Rigid, dominating			
Blame others	Honest, straightforward	Difficult, socially needy, victimized			
Focus on the negative aspects of a situation	Straightforward	Unlikable, unpleasant			
Talk only about extremely positive things	Fun, exciting, upbeat	Unintelligent, insincere, unrealistic			

Expressing Yourself:
The Subtleties of Sex Appeal

The last fundamental is sex appeal. It adds flair to your first impression. Even if you are approachable, warm, and interesting, your interactions will be a little flat if you don't show *at least a little* sexual appeal.

Your sex appeal is much more than sexuality, different from flaunting your body or showing skin. People with the most sex appeal usually don't "put it all out there." If you've ever played the party game "Who would you do?" you know that sex appeal is about more than physical attributes. In this game, a player presents two options to the group of fellow players, such as "Who would you do: Russell Crowe or Tommy Lee Jones?" Then each player must declare who they'd rather be with—hypothetically, of course—and why. You see that the choices often come down to personal allure, confidence, or a sense of playfulness, rather than physical features.

You may feel that sex appeal is something you have or don't have. But it's actually within your control. You can adjust your level of sexual expression to make others feel comfortable around you and to take the relationship to another level—should you choose—to create a closer bond, flirt playfully, or pursue romance. You can leave others with a desire to know more about you and get closer to you. Likewise, if you want to limit the extent of the relationship, you can rein in your sexual expression.

Of course, you show different amounts of sexuality depending on the environment, whether it is a business, social, or romantic setting. But because first meetings are introductory and generally short, the amount of sex appeal you show may not vary tremendously across situations. Your sex appeal is a natural and healthy part of yourself that you display, to some degree, in all settings.

Sex appeal is a sign of your openness and engagement. This chapter outlines the process and style elements of sex appeal. The process is the way you show your appeal—through your appreciation for and attraction to others and with your physical confidence. Your style is how aggressively, passively, or playfully you present your sexuality.

PROCESS: SHOWING YOUR SEX APPEAL

When you think about how you show your sex appeal, you may focus on your body and clothing. But sex appeal is much more than sheer physical beauty. Even supermodels can lack appeal if they lack interest in others or are unresponsive.

You express your sex appeal in many ways. But one of the most important ways is in your appreciation for others—how you react and respond to people. You respond to others with your gaze, with touch, and with your expressions of attraction. You also show your sex appeal with your body and how you inhabit it—in how you show pride and confidence in your physical self.

Appreciation: Responding to Others

We'll start with an important yet underrated element of sex appeal: appreciation for others. It's like a wink—it makes others feel noticed and special. And it's sexy—it makes people want to be around you and get closer to you.

> *A woman is walking down the street on her way to work and sees an attractive man. Their eyes meet, he looks away, but she holds her gaze just a little longer. He notices her glance out of the corner of his eye and sneaks a small smile as he passes by.*

> *A woman is at a professional meeting; she finds the man next to her interesting and fun. She touches him lightly on the arm to whisper a question.*

> *A man is on a first date with a woman. He inquires about her likes and dislikes, asks her opinions, wants to know everything about her. He is engaged and energized.*

Sexuality is about responsiveness. It's showing people, however subtly, that you find them attractive or interesting. This is the essence of flirting. Even if people don't reciprocate your interest, you will likely make them feel good about themselves and thus feel good about you. When you show this attention, it doesn't have to mean that you intend to go any further, and it doesn't have to suggest real sexual or romantic interest. It can be a way of creating a momentary world of "you and me."

So if you are interested in or attracted to someone, and want to show your interest playfully or more seriously, how can you do it on a very first meeting? There are norms as to what is appropriate and comfortable to most people. Some easy ways to show attraction are with eye contact, subtle touch, and special interest and appreciation.

The Window to the Heart

As we described in Chapter 5, making eye contact is one of the most basic ways that we show interest in others. It's also the way we show our attraction to others. If you want to show attraction, you can hold your gaze even longer than usual. People readily notice the extra attention and will feel, almost literally, your extra interest.

TRYING TO IMPRESS THE OTHER SEX

Do you think you make the same effort to impress men as women?

Researchers investigated this question by asking heterosexual participants to keep a diary of their social interactions with people in their everyday life. For each person they interacted with, participants recorded the person's gender and how well they knew the person. They also noted what kind of impression they were trying to make—for example, being likable, competent, or physically attractive—and how they thought they were coming across.

Not surprisingly, participants were concerned with making a positive impression on people they didn't know well. But they were also very concerned with making a positive impression on those of the opposite sex, *even people they knew well.*

The authors hypothesize that cross-sex relationships, even nonromantic ones, may be perceived as more important and less stable than same-sex relationships, and thus stir up more concerns about making positive impressions.

Reaching Out

Another way to show attraction or interest is with touch. In fact, the word "flirt" comes from the French word *fleureter,* meaning "to touch lightly." Touch sends an even more powerful message than gaze. While context matters, most people like to be touched lightly even in

HOW MANY GLANCES DOES
IT TAKE TO GET A MAN?

Women: What does it take to get a man to approach you in a bar? A sly glance? A quick smile?

Researchers set up an experiment in a bar to study this question. A female researcher sat at a table with an attractive woman in her 20s, who served as a research confederate. The researcher picked out a man at least 10 feet away and asked the attractive woman to make eye contact once or multiple times, and to either smile while making eye contact or not. They then waited up to ten minutes to see if the targeted man approached.

Turns out, the men needed a lot of coaxing. One mutual gaze didn't do it, even if she added in a smile. Only the men who had eye contact multiple times combined with a smile were regularly coaxed over (60 percent of the time) to the table. All other combinations worked 20 percent of the time or less.

Even though not all the gazed-upon men approached the woman, they probably noticed her interest, and enjoyed the attention.

nonromantic settings. On a first meeting you can touch others casually as a gesture, to get their attention, or to direct their attention somewhere else. The message usually is: I like you, I am a warm person, I am comfortable with my body. Or it can mean: I want to touch you more. It can be a way of playing a card to see how the other responds.

Interest Begets Attraction

Interest begets interest, as we described in Chapter 5. It's also true that interest begets attraction.

A TOUCHY SUBJECT

Touch, even by a stranger, can have a powerful impact. In general, when a stranger touches you lightly, it has a positive effect on your feeling for that person.

In one study researchers instructed librarians to touch some borrowers for half a second when returning their library cards. Those who were touched reported liking the librarian and the library better, and were in a better mood afterward, than borrowers who were not touched. These positive feelings were elicited regardless of whether the librarian was male or female.

In another study, researchers stopped people in a shopping mall to interview them (allegedly). They touched the shopper somewhere between the shoulder and hand or did not touch them at all. They then dropped some papers and noted whether the person helped to pick them up. They found that touching influenced people to be more helpful and that touching on the arm had the greatest impact. Gender mattered too; female interviewers who touched male shoppers on the upper arm were helped the most.

So, in general, if you touch someone lightly on a first meeting, the person may be warmly predisposed to you.

After a sales conference, a small group of attendees gathered over cocktails to talk about their day. Pauline, a young sales rep, didn't know anyone very well, so she stood quietly and listened to others. Harry, a sales manager, noticed Pauline and tried to draw her into the conversation. He asked her what she thought about the conference speaker and listened to her observations and comments. He said he hadn't thought about some of the speaker's points until she shared her reaction. He told Pauline that she was very insightful. Harry then asked her more about herself, and their talk became lively and fun.

Later that evening, Pauline told a colleague that she found Harry very interesting and attractive.

There is a strong reciprocity in attraction and liking. If you are introduced to three people who are similar in appeal, but learn that one has expressed interest in you, you will like that person more than the others. Pauline was more attracted to Harry than to the other men in the group because he drew her out and showed that he liked her. When you show this kind of attraction, others will likely feel flattered, comfortable around you, and even more attracted to you.

If you are attracted to someone, letting them know how you feel may result in them liking you more. This is one of the biggest "development areas" for our First Impressions clients. They often shrink from showing attraction out of fear of rejection. What they don't realize is that by showing their interest, they actually lessen the probability of rejection.

Of course, you can't make everyone like you or feel romantic attraction to you just by showing that you like them. And going overboard may be off-putting. Nonetheless, you generally have more to gain than to lose by showing your genuine interest.

Comfort in Your Own Skin: Body Emotion

Showing attraction and openness to others is the foundation of sex appeal. But your physical presence matters too. Not just your physical features, but how you feel about your body and how you carry yourself. You may not have a choice in your physical attributes. But you can choose how you present your body. Think of an actor who can be mousy or sexy depending on how he presents himself. He can be Superman or Clark Kent. Same body, different impact. The same is true with you. You can choose how you want to be perceived.

How you feel about yourself shows in how you hold yourself, your posture, and your gait. Like a smile or a yawn, your body emotion is contagious. The way you feel about yourself impacts how others feel about themselves in your presence. If you feel attractive, you present yourself positively. Others will feel good in your presence and thus

YOUR BELIEFS MAY COME TRUE

We like people for many reasons: because they are kind, fun to be around, or interesting. And we tend to dislike them if they are dishonest, boring, and so on. But there is another important factor that determines how much we like someone: how much we think he or she likes us.

In one experiment researchers told participants that another participant either liked them or didn't like them, and then asked them to chat with him or her for ten minutes. The results showed that when participants thought they were liked, they disclosed more personal information, interacted with a warmer attitude and tone of voice, and were less likely to disagree or show differences in feelings than if they thought they were disliked.

Their behavior in turn influenced how much they were liked back. When the participants thought the other person liked them, they actually were liked more in return. When they thought they were disliked, they were disliked more.

Your beliefs may come true. If you think people like you, you'll treat them kindly, and they'll like you more. If you think they don't, it will influence your behavior, and they probably won't like you as much.

find you more attractive. Likewise, when you expect to be found unattractive, others will feel this negative emotion and feel uncomfortable around you. The end result: *You will actually make yourself less attractive.*

Most people are not fully aware of their physical presentation. While you can hear your own voice, you literally can't see your own body and mannerisms the way others do. You know what you look like and what you are wearing. But others notice things about you that you may not. They notice comfort or displaced energy—such

CHARM VERSUS CHEEKBONES

Both beauty and charisma are appealing. And we definitely notice them when we meet someone for the first time. But which affects us more? Which makes someone more appealing or likable?

Psychologists have teased out the answers. They videotaped individuals who were rated on their physical attractiveness and their charisma (emotional expressiveness and social skills) as they entered a room and introduced themselves to two people. They then showed silent videotapes of these interactions to participants and asked them to rate the individual on how likable he or she appeared.

The results showed that attractiveness, emotional expression, and social skills all contributed to likability but that attractiveness contributed the least. In other words, charm won out.

---

as fidgeting or nervous movements. They notice how you feel about yourself.

You show how you feel about yourself by how you inhabit your body and present it to the world. How do you present yourself? Are you comfortable with yourself, or do you feel like you have something you'd like to hide? Do you fully inhabit your body and feel one with it, or does it feel separate from you, or even like a burden? Our clients present their bodies in a variety of ways: They embrace them or cover them up consciously or unconsciously. They show pride or shame. Each approach sends messages about how the person feels about himself—a core element of sex appeal.

Embracing Your Physical Self
Jessica, a small, heavy woman, walked into the café to meet her consultant. Jessica was dressed in a flattering outfit—a tailored skirt and

stylish boots. She sat down across from Nick, introduced herself with a broad smile, and began talking. Nick was charmed by her immediately. Just by the way she presented herself, Jessica sent the message that she was confident, fun, and sexy. She appeared to be content with herself and to expect others to find her appealing. As Nick did.

When Nick gave Jessica feedback about her charm and confidence, Jessica explained that she hadn't always presented herself that way. She used to feel self-conscious about her body. She used to be a little "hyper" when she met new people, a little too loud and energetic, and tried to play the entertainer—to distract people from paying attention to her body. But at some point she realized that when she was confident and relaxed, others responded to her in a different way. She noted that men were much more attracted to her and connected with her more readily when she showed pride in her body and lacked any nervous energy.

Self-Check:

How do others think I feel about my body? Do I appear comfortable in my own skin?

The Comb-over

Some of our clients express their body sensitivities by adjusting their whole presentation around concealing a perceived physical flaw. Take our business client Justin. Justin is a dark-haired man in his early 30s, with a broad build and large eyes. He greeted his consultant with a handshake and a "closed" smile, introduced himself, and offered her a seat. Throughout the conversation, his consultant felt a strange vibe from Justin. He seemed reserved and uncomfortable; he never smiled or relaxed his face completely.

When his consultant addressed his reserve in the feedback session, Justin explained that he really enjoyed the conversation and really liked her. He wasn't smiling because he has crooked teeth; he never flashes a toothy grin because he thinks his smile is unattractive. His consultant helped him to understand that by not smiling appropriately, he sent unintended messages that he didn't like her or that he was socially awkward. When he showed his crooked yet genuine smile, he seemed approachable and appealing.

Self-Check:

Do I have any body sensitivities that I try to compensate for when I meet new people? Am I aware of how I appear when I do so?

Some of our clients pay undue attention to their perceived problem areas, thinking that others will focus on their defects to the same extent they do. Remember the "spotlight illusion" we presented in Chapter 4? People often overestimate how much attention is drawn to physical details. They imagine a spotlight is shining on them. And, like Justin, some people may actually draw more attention to these perceived defects by trying to overcompensate for them.

You may never be totally comfortable with certain aspects of yourself. If you can and want to change them, then do so. But you also can come to accept them and not focus on them. It may seem challenging to overcome long-seated body perceptions and habits, but it's easier than you think. Try acting as if you feel comfortable and attractive, and your beliefs may come true. For example, Justin experimented with smiling broadly when he met new people. When no one reacted in horror, and in fact responded positively, he began to feel at ease with his smile. When he seemed more comfortable in his own skin, he became more appealing to others.

While people may not be able to easily identify it, physical comfort or just the absence of "displaced energy" is attractive. Showing comfort with your body suggests you can be sexually uninhibited and other-oriented, which can actually make you appear sexier to others.

STYLE: YOUR SEXUAL INTENSITY

So far we've talked about the elements of charm and body emotion. They make up the content of your sex appeal. Now we'll turn our attention to your style—how you present your sex appeal to others. Is your style aggressive, passive, or playful? Are you conscious of your style and how others react to it? Most people have a baseline level of sexual display—they fall somewhere on the sexually expressive/sexually restrained continuum—and then adapt to the situation they are in.

Self-Check:

Am I more or less sexually expressive than others in most situations? Do I tend to flaunt or downplay my sexuality? If 10 is extremely sexy, and 1 is not at all, what number describes me?

Your sexuality is part of who you are, whether you are male or female, straight or gay, very feminine or very masculine. *It's how you feel about yourself.* People expect to see some degree of sexual expression in all situations—running errands, at parties, on dates. Even in serious business situations, we usually notice others' sexual expression but just choose not to focus on it or play to it.

If you show some sexuality, even subtly—by the way you look at people or react to them—you will likely make others feel good about themselves and thus good about you, even if they are not aware of why you make them feel that way. It's affirming, even when unexpected. If you show no sexuality at all and are unresponsive to others, you may make others feel, at least unconsciously, that they are unattractive to you. This can be a very subtle or strong rejection, depending on the person or situation. It can make others uncomfortable around you or at least not eager to be in your company.

So how much of your sex appeal should you show on a first meeting? There are no hard and fast rules; it depends on the specific situation. But that said, there are a few ways we have observed people over- or underdo it.

Flaunting: The Aggressive Approach

Scott, a First Impressions client, greeted his consultant with his chest thrust forward. He was wearing a tight-fitting shirt and boots, leaned toward Susan to introduce himself, and took a seat across from her. Throughout the conversation, Scott often drew attention to his body by moving his shoulders and talking about his exercise routine.

In the feedback session, the consultant asked Scott about his body language. Scott said that he works out a lot and likes to show off his body a bit. His consultant pointed out that he did have a sexy body, but by drawing so much attention to it, he sent the message that he had a strong need for sexual attention. She helped Scott to realize that by exhibiting his body so strongly on a first meeting, he may be sending the unintended message that he is either unsatisfied or preoccupied with his physical appearance and sex appeal.

Suppressing: The Passive Approach

Some of our First Impressions clients go in the opposite direction and hold themselves back. Take our client Eddie, an attractive man in his early 40s. Eddie met his date, Susan, in a hotel café. Eddie was skilled in drawing out his date and finding common interests. Despite his charms, however, Susan didn't feel like she was on a date. Instead, she felt like she was having a chummy get-together with a distant cousin. On the surface, Eddie didn't do anything wrong. Rather it was something about his withdrawn body language and "control" that reined in his natural sexuality. He didn't seem to let go physically or emotionally or really be in the moment.

In the feedback session, the consultant told Eddie that she didn't feel like it was a date—that he seemed to be concealing his sexuality or holding himself back. Eddie explained that he is usually uncomfortable on dates and likes to play things very cool.

While safe, this manner can make others feel uncomfortable or bad about themselves in ways that they may not be able to articulate. They may feel that they elicited a cold reaction because they are unattractive or unappealing. Over-controlling your sexual side may limit the extent of your connection to others.

The Playful Approach

Our friend José went on a first date with Jennie, who was chatty and fun. She teased José about his orange shoes. He teased her about being late. She laughed about it. They learned about each other. They pointed out where they agree on things, how they connected.

Jennie's playful style captivated José and brought out his own lighthearted style. They both showed a sense of pleasure in life. The hallmark of this approach to sexual expression is being relaxed and in the moment. It's also about playing off someone. Not only did Jennie and José connect, but they pointed it out to each other. They playfully teased each other and laughed at themselves. They showed confidence and spontaneity.

As we've shown, there are various styles of sexual expression. But as is the general case in first impressions, you'll make others more comfortable if you match your degree of sexual expression to the situation, whether it is a professional meeting or a blind date, and to the person you are with. If you first observe his or her degree of sexual expression and then try to match it, you will most likely send the positive message that you are comfortable to be around. If you want to develop a closer bond with someone, you can try showing a little more of your sexuality and interest, and see if the person matches your move. Then you can adjust yourself accordingly. And, of course, if you want to keep some distance from someone, you can communicate that by holding back your sexual expression.

TOUGH OR TENDER?

When meeting a potential romantic partner, should you show your tough masculine or your sweet feminine side? Or both?

Psychologists have looked at what gender-typed traits people desire in partners for a one-night stand, dating relationship, or marriage. Specifically, they asked participants to rate how desirable they found attractive opposite-sex people who varied in masculine qualities (e.g., independent, competitive, self-confident) and femininity (e.g., emotional, helpful, warm).

The results showed that both men and women prefer people with androgynous characteristics, high in both masculine *and* feminine qualities. And they preferred them across all relationship situations, including one-night stands, dating, and marriage.

So, men and women: Don't be afraid to show both sides of yourself, your confidence and your warmth. They make an appealing combination.

SUMMARY

Sex appeal is more than what you look like and what you wear. It's about showing appreciation for others, having confidence in your body, and presenting a relaxed style of sexual expression. Understanding how you present your sex appeal can give you more control over new relationships, so you may accelerate them or put the brakes on when you want.

Showing your sex appeal is normal and expected in most situations. Holding it back may make others feel that they are unappealing to you or make you seem socially uncomfortable. There are two easy ways to show your sex appeal. Showing appreciation for others is fundamental. Even if you are the most beautiful person in the world, if you don't show an interest and engagement with others, ultimately you won't convey much sex appeal. You can show appreciation and attraction with your eyes, your touch, and your words. The second key element is conveying confidence in your physical self, showing that you accept yourself and that you expect to be found appealing. And finally, you show your sexuality in your style of expression. Being playful and in the moment is sexy. And if you align yourself to the norms of the situation and your conversational partner's comfort, you'll likely be more appealing and comfortable to be with.

How do you show your sex appeal? With your interest, your body, your style? Are you more or less sexually expressive than others? How do others respond to you? You can try experimenting with one of the following behaviors, and see if others react to you differently.

Think about your style while you read through the behaviors. Check off whether you do each behavior usually, sometimes, or rarely.

POSITIVE SEX APPEAL BEHAVIORS

If You Do This:	You May Seem:	Do I Do This?		
		Usually	Sometimes	Rarely
Make appropriate eye contact	Comfortable to be with, socially aware, interested			
Hold your gaze just a little bit longer before looking away	Interested, attracted			
Touch others lightly	Warm, likable, interested			
Openly express your interest or attraction	Interesting, appealing, likable			
Show comfort with your body and an expectation of being found appealing	Appealing, sexy, confident			
Are playful in your interactions with others	Fun, comfortable with yourself, sexy			

COMMON MISCOMMUNICATIONS

If You Do This:	You May Think You Seem:	But You May Seem:	Do I Do This?		
			Usually	Sometimes	Rarely
Make less eye contact than others	Normal, respectful	Rejecting, uninterested, shy, awkward			
Stare	Interested, intense	Threatening, socially inappropriate			
Conceal a body part you are sensitive about	More attractive	Socially awkward, inhibited, self-conscious			
Flaunt your sexuality	Sexy, attractive, approachable	In need of sexual attention or preoccupied with sex			
Conceal your sexuality	Comfortable, nonthreatening	Unattracted to others, rejecting, not sexually inclined			

PART THREE

Tweaking Your First Impression Style

By now you've probably done a lot of thinking about the first impression you make. And you might have some ideas about what you'd like to change—perhaps to introduce more topics, share a little more of yourself, or talk a little bit less. But chances are you're still a bit baffled or unsure about how others see you and what to do about it.

That's what this section is all about: helping you to understand your own first impression style and to learn how to make changes if you desire. We've taken the first impression puzzle apart into its seven fundamentals and helped you look at each piece in detail. Here we show you how to put the pieces back together.

In Chapter 11, we walk you through steps that will help you see your strengths and weaknesses, and compare them to how you would ideally like to come across. Then, in Chapter 12, we help you close the gaps with an easy method we use with our clients. We present practical exercises as well as ways to work through the natural discomfort of speaking and acting differently.

In Chapter 13, we show you what you can do if you make a bad first impression and want to recover. Finally, in Chapter 14, we show you how to use your new knowledge to understand others and cut them a little slack when they make common faux pas with good intentions.

ELEVEN

Awareness: *Do I Do That?*

This is your chance to focus on yourself in detail. You can assess yourself in a number of ways: based on the first impression behaviors presented earlier, what you already know about your areas of sensitivity, and from what people have told you in the past. To learn even more about yourself you can learn to solicit feedback from others.

WHAT KIND OF IMPRESSION DO YOU *ACTUALLY* MAKE?

There are nine steps you can take to illuminate your personal style. Each step includes a self-exploration exercise. A good way to process the information from the exercises is to generate a list of things you've learned about yourself and to jot them down in a "laundry list" style while you are going through the chapter. Take a sheet of paper and write *Strengths* on the left side and *Weaknesses* on the right side. As you think through the exercises in each of the steps, write down one or two things in each column. Don't analyze it yet; later in the chapter we'll show you how to put it together.

STEP 1: KNOW YOUR SOCIAL GIFTS

Let's start with the social gifts you provide to others. Do you make others feel appreciated, connected, elevated, and enlightened? These are the core social benefits we described in Part I. The more of these benefits you give to others, the better the first impression you make. If you deny others these benefits, you may be a social drain and make a less favorable impression.

Many people have a combination of weak and strong suits. For example, someone may be very enlightening and informative, yet not good at recognizing or appreciating others. Someone else may be very connecting, yet not very lively or entertaining.

What about you? What are your strong and weak suits? To assess yourself, take the little test on page 189 and see how balanced you are in social gifts.

All of these behaviors send positive messages, so the areas where you show these behaviors regularly are your strengths. The areas where you have one or more checks in the "sometimes" or "rarely" columns are your weaknesses. Make a note of your stronger and weaker "social gifts" on your list.

STEP 2: EXPLORE YOUR FIRST IMPRESSION FUNDAMENTALS

The seven first impression fundamentals provide another framework for self-assessment: accessibility, showing interest, discussing objective topics, self-disclosure, conversational dynamics, perspective, and sex appeal. Turn back to your self-analyses in the tables at the end of each chapter in Part II. If you just skimmed over the tables while reading, go back and assess yourself now.

If you look at your check marks, you'll find where your strengths lie. Is there one or more fundamental that you are particularly strong in? For example, if you see a lot of checks under the "usually" column for the positive self-disclosure behaviors, then self-disclosure is a

FIRST IMPRESSION BEHAVIORS BY SOCIAL GIFT

When I meet someone new, do I:	Usually	Sometimes	Rarely
Do I make others feel appreciated?			
Do I compliment others on their talents and accomplishments?			
Do I smile and lean toward others when I listen to them?			
Do I ask questions about others?			
Do I listen actively when others speak?			
Do I make others feel connected?			
Do I match my self-disclosures to those of others?			
Do I pay attention to how much people like to speak, and then add a complementary amount?			
Do I share some vulnerabilities and laugh at myself?			
Am I modest about my position relative to others?			
Do I elevate others' mood?			
Do I smile when I meet someone new?			
Do I create a positive mood and draw others out?			
Do I instill energy and emotion in my voice?			
Do I start with positive comments, and save my critical commentary for later?			
Do I enlighten others?			
Do I generate a variety of topics?			
Do I share observations about everyday life?			
Do I share my passions and interests?			
Do I check the urge to talk about the minutiae of my life?			

strength. If in the table on accessibility you send several unintended negative messages, accessibility would be a weakness.

There is no rule as to how many "usually" versus "rarely" checks makes something a strength or a weakness. It's relative to other areas, for you. You may display many positive behaviors on a regular basis, and just have one fundamental where you perform positive behaviors only "sometimes." While that's not bad, it's a weakness for *you*.

So, if you find that you have a fundamental that is an area of strength or weakness, write it down on your list.

STEP 3: IDENTIFY PARTICULAR BEHAVIORS THAT ARE YOUR BEST AND WORST ASSETS

By now you have probably thought, "Oops, I do that" about a few specific behaviors—maybe you realized that you talk a little too much, or that you try to impress others just a bit. These "oops" behaviors may or may not line up under specific "social gifts" or first impression "fundamentals." They may be "stand-alone" gaffes.

Look again at the self-analysis tables from each of the chapters in Part II. Did any one or two behaviors jump out as an "oops"— something you want to change? If so, add them to your list of weaknesses.

STEP 4: REFLECT ON YOUR SECRET SENSITIVITIES

Most of us have some part of ourselves about which we are not completely confident. When faced with a new situation, we may try to conceal or compensate for this perceived weakness. While you may feel that you are coming across well, these compensatory behaviors are often the ones that send unintended negative messages.

For example, if you are insecure about your financial situation—

maybe you earn less than others or were recently laid off—you may try to subtly insert impressive fiscal information, such as a description of a recent purchase, in an effort to compensate. However, it can backfire—you may be more transparent than you think and actually may highlight your area of insecurity. If your sensitivity is with your body image, you may overcompensate by putting on an unnatural personality—one that is louder or softer and much less charming than your natural one.

Do you have an area in which you feel a little insecure or uncomfortable? Most of us do. Do you ever try to compensate for it or conceal it when you meet someone new? Is it possible that you are sending some unintended negative messages? Make a note of any "compensatory" behaviors on your table.

And most of us have some situational sensitivities. Maybe you hate going to your spouse's company parties; you don't remember anyone and don't know what to talk about. Or you hate meeting a new boyfriend's buddies; you feel judged and unsure of yourself. Do you act differently in these situations? What kind of behaviors do you show when you are in a situation that makes you anxious? Do you withdraw, talk too much, or try to posture a bit? Make a note of these situation-specific behaviors.

STEP 5: THINK ABOUT HOW PEOPLE HAVE RESPONDED TO YOU IN THE PAST

Even before you picked up this book, you probably already knew something about your first impression style—your charms as well as your common missteps. In the course of life, people have given you feedback, even though you may not have paid close attention to it or analyzed it (yet). Much of it may be indirect. For example, people give you feedback in the way they respond to you. They may lean toward you when you speak, ask you questions about yourself, or reveal parts of themselves. These are reinforcing signs—signs that you are coming across positively. People may also tell you directly that they like you and even that they liked you from the first time they met you. They may compliment you on your sense of humor, your grace, or your ease of connection.

People may also give you signs when you are not coming across well. For example, they may appear distracted or excuse themselves if you tax their attention span and prattle on too long about something. You have probably noted others' reactions and learned from them in the past. Some people also may have told you directly that their initial impression of you was not as positive as their "later" impression of you. Have you ever had friends or coworkers tell you that they had a different impression of you the first time they met you than they did after having gotten to know you better? Perhaps someone found you distant at first but, after getting to know you, found you to be warm and engaging.

There are probably similarities in how people have responded to you and what they've told you about their first impression of you. What is the common positive feedback and the common ways you have been misinterpreted? Do you know what you did that gave that impression? Was it your body language, what you shared about yourself, or how you responded to them? Again, add these to your list of strengths and weaknesses.

STEP 6: SOLICIT FEEDBACK ABOUT YOUR STYLE

Recalling past feedback is helpful, but it has its limits. Not everyone is comfortable giving feedback, even to a close friend. And people are typically more comfortable giving positive than negative feedback. So it is particularly hard to get honest critical feedback from others—unless you ask, and ask in a constructive way.

Work is a good place to look for feedback on your first impression style. You may learn about your communication style or customer relationship skills from your manager or peers. Progressive companies provide employees with "360-degree surveys" that give employees feedback from everyone around them—superiors, peers, customers, and subordinates. And some companies hire consultants like us to provide detailed, individualized feedback.

You probably have less opportunity to learn about how you present yourself in social situations—for example, when meeting new people at a party. However, you can create that opportunity if you ask for feedback.

Here are some guidelines on good ways to get feedback and to learn from others:

1. Choose a trusted friend who has a style you admire and is sensitive and observant. Explain that you want to learn more about your first impression and interpersonal style.

2. Ask that friend to tell you how you come across when meeting new people for the first time.

3. Encourage her to start by telling you a few positive things you do and then to tell you just one or two things you could do better. Feedback is most productive when it focuses on the positive, but includes just a few constructive observations.

4. Ask your friend to be specific. If she said you were "friendly" or "distant," ask her to tell you exactly what you said or did that made you seem that way. Ask her to point out any gestures or quirks you have.

5. Know that it may be difficult for a friend to give critical feedback. You may want to make her more comfortable by critiquing yourself a bit first, as in "I think I cut people off at times. Have you noticed?"

6. Accept the feedback nondefensively! Don't challenge or deny others' perceptions. Be prepared to hear something you don't know. That's the point of asking. You will learn best if you accept the feedback and thank your friend for the help.

Remember, criticism, even when asked for, is hard to hear. We interact with others in a way that makes sense and feels good to us. Hearing that you may be off-putting can be surprising and painful at first, but it is critical to learning about yourself and moving away from a style that doesn't represent the real you.

And that's what friends are for. Sometimes the only way to gain awareness of particular blind spots is to learn from a friend. We found that many of our clients had no idea that they were sending some unappealing messages. Because they were professionally and socially successful overall, they never understood, until we gave them feedback, that they had one or two behaviors that were off-putting to others.

STEP 7: SYNTHESIS

At this point you may have a list of behaviors under your "strengths" and "weaknesses" columns. Now you can concentrate on synthesizing this information to just one or two things that are meaningful to you.

Start with the good: Look at your written (or mental) notes in the "strengths" column. What are your best first impression features? What are the things that you habitually and naturally do that make a good impression on others? In what ways do you make others feel good about themselves? What especially appealing behaviors come easily to you?

Circle or make note of a few of these that seem most salient to you. Recognize the positive things you do, and remind yourself of them frequently. It's easy to just zoom in on the negative and not acknowledge all the things you do well. These are your charms and your unique appeal; they have been your assets in making friends and having positive relationships. Relying on your positive qualities in a new or uncomfortable situation can make you confident and impressive.

Then think about the "could be better" behaviors: Look at your notes on your first impression weaknesses, things you do that may send unintended negative messages. But before you circle anything or start changing your style, it's very important to review what kind of style you would like to have. Remember, how you present yourself is a very personal choice. It doesn't mean being the way others want you to be, or changing in ways that someone recommends, or even about trying to appeal to more people—*if you don't want to*. How you present yourself should reflect the way *you* want to come across, *your* ideal sense of self.

STEP 8: EXPLORE YOUR "STYLE IDEAL"

How do you *want* to come across? We'll bet you never asked yourself this question directly. But now that you've thought about first impressions in some depth, you can probably answer it. And it's good to think about it before you make any changes to your personal style.

Do you want to be the life of the party? Do you want to appear relaxed and low key? Do you want to make others feel that you care about them, understand them? That you are entertaining, informative? Maybe you want to emphasize one or more of these qualities. Or you may like to provide a solid balance of many of them.

Another way to think about this is to consider people you know who make a great first impression or have an interpersonal style that you admire. Now think of negative role models, people whose styles you don't want to imitate. These positive and negative role models can give you some insight as to your ideal way of presenting yourself. Maybe you aspire to be more like one person you know and less like another.

STEP 9: IDENTIFY THE OBSTACLES TO BEING YOUR IDEAL

Look through your notes in the "weaknesses" column and think about the one or two things you do that prevent you from coming across the way you'd like or from coming across in your ideal way more consistently. Maybe there are small trends, things that surfaced from some of the exercises. Or maybe your weaknesses are separate behaviors that don't fall into a theme.

The important point is to identify what is meaningful *to you*. It may be a miscommunication you never knew about or a foible you've been told about before but never paid much attention to. Or it could be something that you are already good at, but want to be even better at. For example, you may be easy to connect with and comfortable to be around, but want to be able to connect even more readily or more naturally.

We all could be a little better in everything we do. But it's really hard to change everything at the same time. If you try to you may end up frustrated and unable to change anything. So, bearing that in mind, select one thing from your list to develop. It could be what is most important to you, it could be the easiest thing to change, it could be the most fun thing to experiment with. It's up to you.

TWELVE

Closing the Gap

Now that you know what you want to work on, you can move on to the next step: tweaking your style. The "tweaking step" is where you get to experiment, change, and grow from your efforts. It's rewarding, though it can also feel a tad awkward at first—but what new challenge doesn't? If you accept that discomfort is part of the process and keep going, you can have fun with it and actually start to feel liberated from your own habits.

It can be difficult to change your habits if you don't know where to begin. In fact, many of our clients knew they had certain first impression faults, but didn't or couldn't change them because they didn't have an approach. However, tweaking is easy if you follow our simple strategy. The first part is mental—deciding what to change and understanding the emotions involved in change. The second part is active—changing what you say or do, and observing your progress.

STRATEGY: PSYCHING
YOURSELF UP FOR IT

Start with One Behavior

In our professional experience, we've found that people are most successful if they change just one thing at a time. It's like working on your golf swing. If you aim to change many things at the same time—to concentrate on cocking your head a different way, holding your elbow closer, and twisting your left foot a tad—you may end up in the sand pit. It's just too much to think about at once and still hit the ball. The same is true with tweaking your own first impression behaviors. If you try to smile more, adjust your body language, monitor how much you speak, and disclose more of yourself—all at the same time—you may feel overwhelmed and "miss the ball." It's impossible to concentrate on all these behaviors at once and respond to people at the same time.

Pick one behavior. For example, you could concentrate on smiling more—until the time that smiling feels natural and effortless. Then you could turn your attention to tweaking something else, such as adjusting your body language—*so that you only have one challenge in mind at any one time.* Of course, you can develop yourself in many ways. But you will likely have more success and more fun if you take a serial approach—taking on one challenge at a time—rather than a parallel approach—trying to change many things simultaneously.

Keep Your Eye on Others

The tweaking process is even easier if you focus less on the mechanics of what you are doing or changing and more on how it is making others feel. If you are making an effort to smile more when you meet people, watch for the response you get. Since you're only changing one thing at a time, you can see how that particular change impacts others. This feedback lets you monitor your progress.

Prepare for Discomfort

Naturally, the effort of doing something different will make you more aware of how you feel about yourself. It's normal and expected to feel a little awkward at first. Your natural patterns, good or bad, are familiar and comfortable to you. Even when you want to change, you may still feel a gravitational pull back to your regular habits. But discomfort is the only way to change. It's an investment in your future. Trying anything new can be anxiety provoking at first. But, like riding a bike, it gets easier over time and soon can become second nature.

Liberate Yourself from Your Own Habits

Your "first nature" may be based on past situations that no longer exist for you. You might have outgrown that situation, but still have the interpersonal style that you developed at that time. For example, when you were younger, you may have needed to prove yourself to new clients, to demonstrate that you had smart ideas. That may have been critical for getting recognition at that time. However, although you may not need to prove yourself now, you may have retained the tendency to brag a bit about your accomplishments. Or when you were in college, you might have felt inexperienced in life and compensated by talking a lot about your adventures. However, your tales may seem tedious and childish now, rather than entertaining.

Many of the behaviors that seem like your "nature" actually were learned at some point in your life, in reaction to events and people around you. You had to teach yourself those ways of interacting and responding. Personal development means learning different ways of being based on informed choices, not just a reaction to situations.

EXECUTION: ACTUALLY DOING IT

Now that you've prepared yourself mentally, you can jump right in. We recommend you start right away, make a development goal, and monitor your progress.

As a Chinese proverb says, "The longest journey starts with a single step." The same is true with your personal development journey. The first step takes the most effort, the most courage, and may cause the most discomfort. But then each following step is easier and more comfortable.

If you are skittish about taking the first step, you may want to start at the driving range rather than at the big golf tournament. Try making changes in situations that have little consequence to you—for instance, when you are interacting with someone you know you will never see again, such as a stranger on the train or a technical support rep on the phone. It's totally safe. It won't matter if you seem awkward or you over- or underdo it. Like learning any new behavior, it takes a few practice swings to get it right and to feel comfortable. Remember, every first meeting is an opportunity to practice.

Most people find it easy to take small steps and approach change gradually. For example, if you are trying to show more interest in others, you may want to start with the small step of starting the interaction by asking others a single question about themselves. Or you could make the effort to ask one more question than you normally do or to listen just a little longer before sharing your own experience.

Some people like a bolder approach. They like taking bigger steps. If you want to show more interest in others, a big step may mean experimenting with not talking about your own ideas or experiences *at all*—suppressing that desire and focusing only on the other person. Or if you would like to self-disclose more, you may decide to open up and share something sensitive about yourself at the onset of the conversation.

Taking big steps means temporarily exaggerating in the other direction to see how it feels and see how people respond to you. After you develop some comfort with the extreme, you can find a balance that represents how you would like to come across.

Try Out Your New Tricks

This is really important: Start now. Find an opportunity to try out your first impression tweak today. It may not mean taking any extra time out of your day. It can just be making a small change to an interaction that would happen anyway. You can also create opportunities—you can take the initiative to strike up a conversation or introduce yourself to someone. You have opportunities all around you to try out your new behavior. You can banter with a grocery store clerk, smile at the UPS delivery person, chat with your airplane seatmate, or connect with the new temp in the office.

Starting immediately is critical. If you wait for the right situation or for some special first meeting, you may never do it. We've found that the biggest obstacle to personal development that our clients experience is not a lack of desire or resistance to change, but rather a hesitancy to get started.

CHARTING YOUR PROGRESS

Make a Goal

Set a specific goal. But be sure it's one that you are *absolutely certain* you can reach. Having a goal makes it easier to focus—and will encourage you in your pursuits. When you reach your goal, you can set a higher one.

There are different kinds of goals. One goal could be to perform a new behavior to a certain degree or with a certain frequency. Another goal could be to observe certain kinds of feedback. For example, if you would like to yield more of the floor to others and not dominate conversations, you could choose one of the following goals:

- The next time I meet someone new, I will try to listen at least 60 percent of the time and talk only 40 percent of the time.
- I will practice not dominating the conversation at least once every other day.
- I will observe the way others respond to me when I speak less— and see if they seem more comfortable around me.

You could use one of these goals, a variant of it, or another goal that is meaningful to you. Write it down, enter it in your PDA, make a mental note, tell a friend, or whatever you need to do to make it real, and commit yourself to it. Your specific goal is a personal choice based on how you like to develop and how comfortable you are with change. It can be based on how big a step you take, how often you try your new behavior, how others respond to you, or a date by which you intend to have made progress.

Reassess Yourself

To chart your progress periodically, you can:

- Review the self-test charts and check whether you demonstrate that specific behavior usually, sometimes, or rarely.
- Note how others respond to you when you show your new first impression style; for example, do people smile back? Do they laugh?
- Ask a trusted friend for feedback. Ask him or her to tell you when you are coming across well and modeling your new behavior, and when you are falling back to your old style. To get the most out of this information, review the guidelines for soliciting feedback in Chapter 11.
- Measure yourself relative to your goals. For example, are you challenging yourself to try your new behavior every other day?
- Notice your personal comfort. Is your new behavior still uncomfortable, or has it become effortless and natural?

If you are making progress and meeting your goal, you can raise the bar. That is, you can set even more challenging goals, such as trying the new behavior every day rather than once a week, or practicing it 90 percent of the time, until it is natural and habitual.

TAKING ON ANOTHER

When you have comfortably integrated your first impression tweak into your natural style, you can turn your attention to another area to develop. Was there another behavior you'd like to improve on? If so, you can repeat this process. Now that you know the steps involved and feel rewarded for your efforts, you will feel empowered to develop any way you want. Just remember to focus on only one challenge at a time, set small goals, and pace your changes in a way that feels comfortable to you.

THIRTEEN

Sometimes It Happens:
Overcoming a Bad First Impression

Now you've done all the exercises and put all your first impression behaviors into practice. You're feeling confident in your new skills. Then it happens, as it does to everyone. Something goes awry and you make a bad first impression. Or at least one you weren't intending. Maybe you were distracted and didn't carry your share of the conversation, or you got excited by some topic and talked too much about it, or you were so enamored of someone that you lost your composure.

Can you overcome it? The answer in many cases is yes. But remember: People make assumptions about you based on your initial behavior and then are biased to see you in this way. So you are working against this bias. How long it takes to overcome this bias will depend on the situation, the nature of your gaffe, and the opportunities for future interactions.

But there are some ways to turn the situation around. Here we show you how you can overcome an initial gaffe and improve your overall impression.

Take the example of Henry and Megan:

Henry and Megan are seated next to each other at a dinner.

Megan turns to Henry and asks him if he is enjoying his meal. Henry is slow to speak; he clears his throat and then comments that he loves the carrot soup. Megan asks him if he is a vegetarian. Henry explains, "No, but I love vegetables," but before he finishes, Megan jumps in to ask about his background and where he was born. The conversation continues like this until Henry, feeling interrogated and overwhelmed, finds an opportunity to join in a conversation with the person sitting across from him.

Megan didn't make a great first impression on Henry. She came across as aggressive and insensitive, and Henry didn't enjoy her company. Megan realized that something went wrong. Henry seemed to avoid talking to her and later left without saying good-bye. Megan accepted that she made a bad first impression on Henry. But she wondered, "What should I do?"

If something similar happens to you, we recommend that you first reflect on the experience. If you make a bad impression or if someone reacts negatively to you, it doesn't mean you have to hustle to repair your impression. Ask yourself if you were comfortable with the way you behaved and whether it reflected the real you. If you were comfortable with yourself, you can choose to let it go. No one can please and connect with everyone, and if someone doesn't like your style, it may mean that he is not a good personality match for you.

For example, Megan may be a high-energy woman who enjoys the company of people who jump quickly into conversations and match her speed and intensity. She may like that quality in herself. Henry may not be someone she would have much fun interacting with. In this case, Megan could leave the situation feeling comfortable with herself and okay with the fact that she and Henry didn't hit it off.

But if Megan wasn't pleased with how she came across or really wanted to make a connection with Henry, she could try to overcome her initial bad impression. She could address it directly, by acknowledging her first impression flaw before, during, or after the encounter. Or she could overcome it indirectly—by revealing her natural charms over time or by being extra socially generous in the future.

DIRECT APPROACHES

Heads-up

A "heads-up" is stopping a bad impression before it starts—it's a preemptive approach. If you know that some situations make you uncomfortable or cause you to behave differently than you usually do, you can explain that tendency up front. It's like telling someone "Bear with me, this isn't the real me." For example, if you know you can be shy with new people, when arranging a blind date you can say "By the way, I just want to let you know I am often a little quiet the first time I meet someone." Or, if you know you tend to get talkative when you are overtired, you can tell your new acquaintance, "I'm exhausted today, and sometimes that makes me verbose. I hope I don't carry on too much." Of course, not every situation lends itself to a heads-up warning. But if appropriate, a heads-up can head off a bad first impression. It opens others' eyes to seeing the you beyond your initial jitters.

Stop It in Its Tracks

Here you stop a bad impression before it's fully formed. If you notice that things are going awry or that others are not reacting to you as you would like, you can try to correct your impression in its tracks. For example, if Megan knew she had a tendency to question new people aggressively and caught herself doing it, she could have backed off and said, "I'm sorry, go on, what were you saying?" She also could have apologized and said, "I tend to ask too many questions sometimes. Sorry! So, you were saying..." This would have given Megan the opportunity to show Henry a better side of herself and to keep the door open to making a positive impression.

The Postimpression Jump Start

Even after an interaction goes badly, you can still recover. One way is with a direct apology and request for a second chance. This is a tricky one. It's not a great idea if you don't expect to see the person again. For example, if Henry and Megan were merely guests at a party, it would be awkward for Megan to track him down to apologize and ask to make it up to him, as in "Gee, I came on a little strong, but I promise I'm not always like that. Would you give me a second chance, just a quick drink or something?" Megan would probably look needy and even aggressive.

However, if Megan was likely to see Henry again—if, for example, they were new coworkers, had close mutual friends, or lived in the same neighborhood, then the jump-start approach could help. Let's say Megan and Henry are new coworkers, and it is important to Megan that she make up for her bad impression. She could send Henry a short follow-up e-mail or voice message in which she admits her blunder and asks to make it up to him. For instance, she could say, "I enjoyed meeting you. But I think the excitement of the dinner got to me, and I didn't give you the chance to talk. Next time we meet I promise I'll be more low key, and I'd love to hear more about you." It's good form to leave a message, so that Henry does not feel put on the spot.

While the jump-start approach may seem awkward, it can turn things around. In this example, Megan would show self-awareness and humility and an interest in connecting with Henry. She may overcome her initial bad impression more quickly than if she did nothing. People sometimes react more positively and are more forgiving when you convey your awareness of your impact on them. It's also a good approach to use if you do something particularly egregious or embarrassing—such as insulting the host or dancing on the table!

These direct approaches involve an acknowledgment of your first impression flaw, an implicit or explicit request for forgiveness, and a promise that it doesn't reflect how you behave most of the time. Of course, these direct methods will work only if you actually deliver on your promise and correct your behavior the next time. If you say "I don't always talk so much" and then talk nonstop on the second meeting, you only dig yourself in deeper.

And if you don't know specifically what you did that was off-putting, it's harder to apologize. All you can say is that you are sorry things didn't go more smoothly. If you don't know your gaffe, you can gain insight by self-reflecting, considering your common miscom-

MEETINGS WITH A FUTURE

Not all first meetings are alike. Sometimes you meet someone and expect to see him again, as with a new coworker. Sometimes you meet someone and have no expectation of seeing him again, as in a casual meeting on a train. Do you think you act differently in "meetings with a future" than in "meetings with no future"?

Psychologists have looked at the differences between these two types of meetings. In one study, two participants were asked to speak with each other for five minutes; some were told they would meet the person the following week, and some were not.

Surprisingly, the participants didn't act differently or share different kinds of information whether they had a future meeting or not. But they evaluated themselves differently. When they expected to see the person again, they were more critical of themselves. They felt that the information they shared was less important and less interesting than their partner felt it was. They also thought their information was less interesting than what the other person spoke of. When participants didn't expect to see the person again, they thought their information was superior to their partners': more important, interesting, and clear.

So when you meet a new coworker, you are probably more interesting than you think. On the other hand, your seatmate on the train may not find you as dazzling as you think you came across.

munications, or asking someone who was present to share her perceptions. If you're still not sure, you can try the indirect recovery methods.

The indirect approaches work whether you know what your gaffe was or not. With these methods, you don't openly acknowledge your error or apologize. Rather, you recover over time and with social attention and generosity. Of course, these approaches work only with people with whom you have ongoing opportunities to interact.

INDIRECT APPROACHES

Letting Time Tip the Scale

After you make a bad impression, others will initially be biased toward seeing you in a negative light. However, over time, the natural positive behaviors you reveal ultimately may outweigh your one initial bad behavior.

Patience is key. But be confident in the fact that if you have enough opportunities, and display your natural charms in subsequent meetings, the scale will likely tip in your favor.

You can usually endear yourself if you show a little extra attention and respect to your new acquaintance. You can point out what you appreciate about the person, as long as it's not done in a blatantly obsequious way. And remember the four social gifts from Part I. Think about whether you are providing your offended acquaintance with appreciation, connection, elevation, and entertainment. Focus on satisfying his social needs. And strive to be at your interpersonal best in future encounters.

If Megan has ongoing interactions with Henry in the workplace, she may get a chance to show him that she is really kind and interesting, not an overbearing person. Little by little, Henry may come to see her in a different light, and she may overcome her initial bad impression.

Tipping the Scale with Social Generosity

If you want to repair your impression more quickly, you can take a proactive approach. You can tailor your subsequent behaviors in a way that makes the other person more comfortable around you. The trick here is to figure out your offended acquaintance's personal style and to adapt your style to his. You probably know how to do this and do it naturally in your conversations with people you know well. It is just being extra attentive and extra socially generous.

First, pay attention to the person's social and stylistic preferences. What does he seem to like in social interactions? Understand his needs, and then provide them. If he likes to talk about facts and new information, focus your conversations on new things you've learned. If he likes to find connection, reveal more about yourself and point out what you have in common.

Observe his dynamic style and synchronize with it. If he likes to speak slowly, speak slowly too, even if it's not your natural speed. Also, notice how much he likes to speak and speak a complementary amount. If he speaks a lot, speak less, again regardless of your preference. Remember, making a good impression is about meeting others' needs, not your own. As the relationship recovers, you can show more of your own style and find a more mutually satisfying dynamic.

If Megan has ongoing opportunities to interact with Henry, she could pay more attention to satisfying his social desires and adapting to the way he likes to speak. For example, if Henry likes entertaining interactions, she could engage him in lighthearted banter. She could note that he likes to talk at a slower pace than she does and slow her speech to match his. She could observe how much he likes to speak and speak a complementary amount.

In this way, Megan may win Henry's favor more quickly than by letting time tip the scales. It still takes time. But it can make her subsequent interactions go more smoothly and accelerate her recovery.

SUMMARY

We all make bad first impressions, at least occasionally; it's part of being human. Sometimes your bad impression is just a bad fit with someone and not something you necessarily want to address. Not everyone is going to like you, and that's okay. But if you do want to make a positive connection, you can overcome your initial negative behavior. With a little effort and patience, you can build a positive relationship.

Whether and how you choose to repair your impression will depend on the specifics of the situation: how important the connection is to you, the opportunities for future interactions, and the nature of your misstep. Of course, there is no guarantee that you will be able to overcome all bad impressions. Sometimes you won't have the chance to see the person again, and some people are just unforgiving. In these cases, you can accept the reaction and move on. You can learn from your experience and avoid making the same first impression blunder again.

FOURTEEN

Cutting Others Slack

Your knowledge of first impressions gives you another edge: It allows you to judge people more fairly. As we've outlined in Parts I and II, first impressions can be inaccurate. People often feel uncomfortable when meeting someone new, and this discomfort may manifest itself in behaviors that are not necessarily typical of their general behavior. Have you ever gotten to like someone who made a bad first impression? Probably not often. Usually we don't seek out the company of people who made a bad first impression. We may never interact with them again unless we are obliged to, because the person is a neighbor or a coworker, for example.

How many people have you misjudged, or even rejected, before getting to see their real selves and true charms? You can use your first impression insights to better understand what others are trying to communicate. You may find that some things that turn you off are in fact signs of interest and affection. You can transcend some of your hasty initial judgments.

Your new knowledge can also allow you to change the tone of an interaction. You can turn a boring or frustrating situation into a more mutually satisfying one. And you can open yourself up to future positive experiences.

REVERSE ENGINEERING

Always consider the person's intentions. The perceptions outlined in Part II represent typical ways in which people process behavioral information. For example, people who share their vulnerabilities may be perceived as confident. People who talk in great detail about themselves may be seen as self-absorbed. However, those perceptions may or may not represent the person's true nature. If these people *consistently* display these behaviors, they may indeed have the personality traits connected to them.

But you can't make that call the first time you meet someone! You haven't had the opportunity to see patterns yet. And first meetings often bring out atypical behavior in people. So you may want to consider the possible intentions in the way people act and give them the benefit of the doubt. You may find out that some off-putting behaviors are really indirect signs of interest in you.

Remember the tables in Part II where we discuss intended and unintended messages? Now, by reversing the code, you can consider the other person's intentions. For example, if someone starts sharing a lot of heavy personal information on a first meeting, you might initially think that that person is needy or self-absorbed. But if you use your first impression insights, you may realize that the person may be communicating that he feels comfortable with you and is open and honest, and wants to connect with you further. If someone leans away from you and doesn't smile, you may think he is arrogant or uninterested, when he may actually be curious about you, but shy and uncertain in first meetings. In this table we highlight the possible good intentions in some unappealing behavior.

What Others May Do	How You May Perceive Them	What They May Intend
Volunteer impressive information	Needy of affirmation, egotistical	Interested in you, wanting to be liked
Lecture you on a topic they know well	Self-important, boring	To appear interesting to you, to inform and entertain
Respond in great detail	Self-absorbed, boring, insensitive	To show their enthusiasm, engagement in life
Wait for an introduction	Distant, uncomfortable, uninviting, passive	Neutral, unobtrusive
Fail to smile	Uninterested, having a negative disposition	Natural, observant
Speak more loudly than others	Bombastic, self-satisfied, offensive	Self-confident, fun, interesting
Fail to yield the floor	Self-focused, difficult to connect with	Interesting, informative

REVERSING THE FILTER: KNOW YOUR BIASES

Remember the first impression filter we described in Part I? Here's how you form an image of others:

1. You take in initial information about people—you notice their body language, what they say, and how they respond.
2. Based on this initial information, you form an impression of them—making assumptions about what they are like and how they will behave in the future.
3. Then you see them through this filter. Like everyone, you believe yourself to be a good judge of character. You look for

information that is consistent with your first impression, and you don't pay a lot of attention to or even ignore behavior that doesn't fit your impression.

Some Common Filtering Errors

Everyone makes common errors when filtering information about others. If you are aware of these errors, you are in a better position to minimize them.

You make the *fundamental error of attribution* when you attribute a person's specific behavior to his general personality, rather than an external or temporary situation. To overcome this, you might try to remember that situations play a big role in how people feel and behave, and look around for external triggers. If someone you meet in the workplace acts distant and unfriendly, consider that he might have just gotten some upsetting news or have been chewed out by the boss before making a judgment about his personality. If someone sitting next to you at a dinner party seems aloof, you may consider that she is preoccupied with something that someone just said to her or that she is not feeling well before writing her off as haughty. You can also be proactive and ask someone how he is feeling or how his day was—and you may find out what's behind his unwelcoming behavior.

Another filtering bias is *cluster illusions,* which is when you assume that certain behaviors or traits are linked, as in the halo and horns effects. For example, if you observe someone being impolite, you may assume that he is also self-centered, unintelligent, and weak, even though you have not observed these qualities in him, and they may not be true. The guy may be ill-mannered as well as kind, smart, and generous. Keep this in mind, and check a tendency to see someone as "all good" or "all bad."

Your Unique Biases

While errors of attribution and the halo and horns effects are common to most people, each of us has some personal experiences and preferences that bias our perceptions in idiosyncratic ways.

My Own Stereotype: She Reminds Me of Someone I Know
We all have unique life experiences that color our perceptions. Much as we may adore or hate the name "Claudia" or "Brian" because of our experience with people with that name, we have "personal stereotypes" about certain behaviors. For example, you may think people with an accent like your former boss's are mean, people with a smile like your grandmother's are loving, people who talk about themselves like your brother-in-law does are pompous, people who interrupt like your ex-girlfriend are psychotic—when it's not true.

Certain behaviors may remind you of others in your life and trigger a whole cluster of assumptions more related to the person you know than to your new acquaintance. Other people may not judge your new acquaintance in the same manner. While you may not be able to rid yourself of all these biases, you can lessen the severity of your judgment. The first step in "debiasing" yourself is awareness. If you are aware of a strong reaction to someone, ask yourself if the person reminds you of someone in your life. Then you can try to dissociate your feelings for the new person from your "personal stereotypes."

Too Close to Home: He Reminds Me of . . . Me
Some things people do may hit a hot button about something you are personally sensitive about—a sensitivity that you struggle with or that you overcame. You may react strongly to people who bring up something you haven't resolved in yourself; for example, you might have a bad feeling about someone you meet who is successful in music if you aspired to be a musician but never fulfilled your dream. Or you may be overly judgmental of people who have a weakness that you overcame, yet still feel sensitive about. For example, you may be judgmental of people who misuse words in ways you used to, or smokers, if you are an ex-smoker.

You can overcome this bias if you pay attention to reactions that stem from a personal issue. If you notice this, you may actually be able to turn a negative reaction into a positive one—realizing that you share similarities with the person.

BIASED BY YOUR OWN DISTRACTION

Along with some of the psychological predispositions to making errors in judgments, researchers have found that a simple lack of attention can cause misperceptions. One study examined the kinds of impressions people formed when they were confronted with attention-grabbing distractions while interviewing someone. The findings showed that interviewers who were very distracted and unable to carefully attend to the person they were interviewing were ultimately biased in their approach. They asked leading questions that fulfilled false expectations they had been given prior to the interview. This happened in spite of the interviewers' intentions and efforts to be unbiased.

What does this mean for you? If you are distracted, either with self-monitoring or other concerns, you will more likely be biased in the way you see other people. If your mind is clear, you will likely see them more accurately. So you may just want to be more lenient toward those you meet when you are busy or distracted.

CHANGING THE COURSE

Even if you are put off by a behavior or two, you don't have to let the other person determine the tone of the interaction. If you remain pleasant instead of reacting to the person's grumpiness or arrogance, you may elevate her mood and engage in a fun conversation. If you focus on making her feel comfortable and understood, she may return the attention.

You can turn a neutral or even unpleasant interaction into a positive one by taking the initiative to change it. If, for instance, you are bored listening to someone lecture you, stop asking questions. See if he changes the topic. If you are tired of waiting to be asked something, volunteer the information and see where things go from there. If someone is very anxious and you find your own blood pressure rising by the second, try using your sense of humor to reduce the tension. Or change the subject to something that you both may find more soothing and relaxing.

LETTING GO OF A GRUDGE

Despite your first impression insights, it's inevitable that some people will leave you with a negative impression. Maybe a new coworker brags in an irritating way about his recently purchased Humvee, and you write him off as a jerk. Later he may behave with grace—he may ask about your family, compliment you on your work, and share some of his vulnerabilities. But as we described in Chapter 13, it can take time for him to overcome his bad first impression. Because you are still thinking about the time he blabbered about his Humvee, you might not be open to seeing his charming qualities.

But holding on to a bad impression is like holding a grudge. It's like refusing to see the other person's full value or perspective and not yielding out of pride of one's conviction. If you think of your first impression not as a conviction or a position to defend, but a starting point in a path to understanding someone, you'll see people in a more nuanced manner.

Look to *disconfirm* someone's bad first impression. Remind yourself that this person has an entire life that you know nothing about, and he most likely has some lovable qualities and interesting life perspectives. Then you'll notice things about him that you didn't see at first. Maybe you'll see that your Humvee-owning coworker has a dry and creative sense of humor. Maybe he does tai chi; maybe he used to be a pastry chef, or spent two years in Ghana in the Peace Corps.

SUMMARY

Withholding judgment isn't easy, but it can be done. It amounts to challenging yourself to not let immediate feelings shut the door on someone. And there is a payoff to you. You may open yourself up to many more fun and interesting social experiences and develop unexpected friendships and relationships.

If you give someone a *second chance,* she might make a good *first impression.*

Conclusion

Every time you cross paths with someone, you affect him or her and are affected in return. You have the power to make it a positive, negative, or life-altering influence. It's a choice you make.

I have come to the frightening conclusion that I am the decisive element. It is my personal approach that creates the climate. It is my daily mood that makes the weather. I possess tremendous power to make life miserable or joyous. I can be a tool of torture or an instrument of inspiration, I can humiliate or humor, hurt or heal. In all situations, it is my response that decides whether a crisis is escalated or de-escalated, and a person is humanized or de-humanized.

—GOETHE

References

Chapter 4. Opening the Door: Accessibility

Most Like It Hot
R. Gifford, "A Lens-Mapping Framework for Understanding the En-coding and Decoding of Interpersonal Dispositions in Nonverbal Behavior," *Journal of Personality and Social Psychology,* 66, no. 2 (1994): 398–412.

The Spotlight Illusion
T. Gilovich, V. H. Medvec, and K. Savitsky, "The Spotlight Effect in Social Judgment: An Egocentric Bias in Estimates of the Salience of One's Own Actions and Appearance," *Journal of Personality and Social Psychology,* 78, no. 2 (2000): 211–222.

The Warp Speed of Emotional Expression
N. Ambady and R. Rosenthal, "Thin Slices of Expressive Behavior as Predictors of Interpersonal Consequences," *Psychological Bulletin,* 111, no. 2 (1992): 256–274.

The Chicken or the Egg?
F. Strack, L. L. Martin, and S. Stepper, "Inhibiting and Facilitating Conditions of the Human Smile: A Non-Obtrusive Test of the Facial Feedback Hypothesis," *Journal of Personality and Social Psychology,* 54, no. 5 (1988): 768–777.

Handshake Messages
W. F. Chaplin, J. B. Phillips, J. D. Brown, N. R. Clanton, and J. L. Stein, "Handshaking, Gender, Personality, and First Impressions," *Journal of Personality and Social Psychology,* 19, no. 4 (2000): 110–117.

Chapter 5. Enough about Me: Showing Interest

Shifty Eyes
J. K. Burgoon, D. A. Coker, and R. A. Coker, "Communicative Effects of Gaze Behavior: A Test of Two Contrasting Explanations," *Human Communications Research,* 12, no. 4 (1986): 495–524.
Liking Your Observer
C. L. Kleinke and C. Taylor, "Evaluation of Opposite-Sex Person as a Function of Gazing, Smiling, and Forward Lean," *Journal of Social Psychology,* 131, no. 3 (1990): 451–453.
More about Me: Conversational Narcissism
A. L. Vangelisti, M. L. Knapp, and J. A. Daly, "Conversational Narcissism," *Communication Monographs,* 57 (1990): 251–274.
Flattery Will Get You Far
R. Vonk, "Self-Serving Interpretations of Flattery: Why Ingratiation Works," *Journal of Personality and Social Psychology,* 82, no. 4 (2002): 515–526.
"Sucking Up" at Work
R. A. Gordon, "Impact of Ingratiation on Judgments and Evaluations: A Meta-Analytic Investigation," *Journal of Personality and Social Psychology,* 71, no. 1 (1996): 54–70.

Chapter 6. Pass the Topic: The Subject Matter of First Conversations

Attitudes of Attraction
J. W. Condon and W. D. Crano, "Inferred Evaluation and the Relation between Attitude Similarity and Interpersonal Attraction," *Journal of Personality and Social Psychology,* 54, no. 5 (1988): 789–797.
A Recipe for Boredom
M. A. Leary, P. A. Rogers, R. W. Canfield, and C. Coe, "Boredom in Interpersonal Encounters: Antecedents and Social Implications," *Journal of Personality and Social Psychology,* 52, no. 5 (1986): 968–975.

Topic Tools
    K. Kellermann, S. Broetzmann, T.-S. Lim, and K. Kitao, "The Conversation Mop: Scenes in the Stream of Discourse," *Discourse Processes,* 12 (1989): 27–61.
Secrets of Skilled Conversationalists
    W. Douglas, "Initial Interaction Scripts: When Knowing Is Behaving," *Human Communication Research,* 11, no. 2 (1984): 203–219.

Chapter 7. Showing Your Cards: Self-Disclosure

Sharing and Liking
    N. L. Collins and L. C. Miller, "Self-Disclosure and Liking: A Meta-Analytic Review," *Psychological Bulletin,* 116, no. 3 (1994): 457–475.
My Friend Once Met Madonna
    R. B. Cialdini and M. E. Nicholas, "Self-Presentation by Association," *Journal of Personality and Social Psychology,* 57, no. 4 (1989): 626–631.
Respect or Rapport
    D. Tannen, *You Just Don't Understand* (New York: Ballantine Books, 1990).
    D. R. Shaffer and J. K. Ogden, "On Sex Differences in Self-Disclosure During the Acquaintance Process: The Role of Anticipated Future Interactions," *Journal of Personality and Social Psychology,* 51, no. 1 (1986): 92–101.
Another Recipe for Boredom
    M. A. Leary, P. A. Rogers, R. W. Canfield, and C. Coe, "Boredom in Interpersonal Encounters: Antecedents and Social Implications," *Journal of Personality and Social Psychology,* 52, no. 5 (1986): 968–975.

Chapter 8. Got Rhythm? Conversational Dynamics

I Like the Way You Move
    R. E. Riggio and H. S. Friedman, "Impression Formation: The Role of Expressive Behavior," *Journal of Personality and Social Psychology,* 50, no. 2 (1986): 421–427.
Just My Speed
    S. Feldstein, F.-A. Dohm, and C. L. Crown, "Gender and Speech Rate in the Perception of Competence and Social Attractiveness," *Journal of Social Psychology,* 141, no. 6 (2001): 785–806.

Harmonizing Bodies
J. N. Cappella, "Behavioral and Judged Coordination in Adult Informal Social Interactions: Vocal and Kinesic Indicators," *Journal of Personality and Social Psychology,* 72, no. 1 (1997): 119–131.
T. L. Chartrand and J. A. Bargh, "The Chameleon Effect: The Perception-Behavior Link and Social Interaction," *Journal of Personality and Social Psychology,* 76, no. 6 (1999): 893–910.
Interrupters: Friend or Foe?
C. A. Chambliss and N. Feeny, "Effects of Sex of Subject, Sex of Interrupter, and Topic of Conversation on the Perception of Interruptions," *Perceptual and Motor Skills,* 75 (1992): 1235–1241.

Chapter 9. How You See the World: Perspective

Your Body and Your Status
A. Leffler, D. L. Gillespie, and J. C. Conaty, "The Effects of Status Differentiation on Nonverbal Behavior," *Social Psychology Quarterly,* 45, no. 3 (1982): 153–161.
The Invisible Influence
J. D. Vorauer and D. T. Miller, "Failure to Recognize the Effect of Implicit Social Influence on the Presentation of Self," *Journal of Personality and Social Psychology,* 73, no. 2 (1997): 281–295.
You're Glue
J. J. Skowronski, D. E. Carlston, L. Mae, and M. T. Crawford, "Spontaneous Trait Transference: Communicators Take on the Qualities They Describe in Others," *Journal of Personality and Social Psychology,* 74, no. 4 (1998): 837–848.

Chapter 10. Expressing Yourself: The Subtleties of Sex Appeal

Trying to Impress the Other Sex
M. R. Leary, J. B. Nezlek, D. Downs, J. Radford-Davenport, J. Martin, and A. McMullen, "Self-Presentation in Everyday Interactions: Effects of Target Familiarity and Gender Composition," *Journal of Personality and Social Psychology,* 67, no. 4 (1994): 664–673.
How Many Glances Does It Take to Get a Man?
D. G. Walsh and J. Hewitt, "Giving Men the Come-on: Effect of Eye

Contact and Smiling in a Bar Environment," *Perceptual and Motor Skills,* 61 (1985): 873–874.

A Touchy Subject

J. D. Fisher, M. Rytting, and R. Heslin, "Hands Touching Hands: Affective and Evaluative Effects of Interpersonal Touch," *Sociometry,* 39 (1975): 416–421.

S. Paulsell and M. Goldman, "The Effect of Touching Different Body Areas on Prosocial Behavior," *Journal of Social Psychology,* 122 (1984): 269–273.

Your Beliefs May Come True

R. C. Curtis and K. Miller, "Believing Another Likes or Dislikes You: Behaviors Making the Beliefs Come True," *Journal of Personality and Social Psychology,* 51, no. 2 (1986): 284–290.

Charm versus Cheekbones

H. S. Friedman, R. E. Riggio, and D. F. Casella, "Nonverbal Skill, Personal Charisma, and Initial Attraction," *Personality and Social Psychology Bulletin,* 14, no. 1 (1988): 203–211.

Tough or Tender?

B. L. Green and D. T. Kenrick, "The Attractiveness of Gender-Typed Traits at Different Relationship Levels: Androgynous Characteristics May Be Desirable After All," *Personality and Social Psychology Bulletin,* 20, no. 3 (1994): 244–253.

Chapter 13. Sometimes It Happens: Overcoming a Bad First Impression

Meetings with a Future

K. Kellermann, "Anticipation of Future Interaction and Information Exchange in Initial Interaction," *Human Communications Research,* 13, no. 1 (1986): 41–75.

Chapter 14. Cutting Others Slack

Biased by Your Own Distraction

J. C. Biesanz, S. L. Neuberg, D. M. Smith, T. Asher, and T. N. Judice, "When Accuracy-Motivated Perceivers Fail: Limited Attention Resources and the Reemerging Self-Fulfilling Prophecy," *Personality and Social Psychology Bulletin,* 20, no. 5 (2001): 621–629.

Index

234 | Index

About the Authors

ANN DEMARAIS, Ph.D., and VALERIE WHITE, Ph.D., are the founders of First Impressions, Inc., a unique consulting firm that helps clients understand how they are perceived on first dates and in social situations, as well as consultants to managers in Fortune 100 companies on communication and leadership skills. They and First Impressions, Inc., have been featured in newspapers and magazines around the world and over such radio and television broadcast outlets as NPR, BBC, Public Radio International, *20/20,* CBS, and Lifetime, among others. The authors live in the New York metropolitan area. Visit them at www.firstimpressionsconsulting.com.